D0394536

what i learned from

a simple blessing

ZONDERVAN

A Simple Blessing
Copyright © 2011 by Michael W. Smith

This title is also available as a Zondervan ebook.
Visit www.zondervan.com/ebooks.

This title is also available in a Zondervan audio edition.
Visit www.zondervan.fm.

Requests for information should be addressed to:
Zondervan, *Grand Rapids, Michigan* 49530

Library of Congress Cataloging-in-Publication Data

Smith, Michael W. (Michael Whitaker)
    A simple blessing : the extraordinary power of an ordinary prayer / Michael W. Smith with
Thomas Williams.
        p.   cm.
    ISBN 978-0-310-32756-1 (hardcover, jacketed)
    1. Christian life. 2. Blessing and cursing. I. Williams, T. M. (Thomas Myron), 1941- II. Title.
BV4501.3.   S6543 — 2010
248.32 — dc22   201003978

Published in association with Chaz Corzine and Greg Ham, The MWS Group, Franklin, Tennessee.

Packaged by Worthy Media. For subsidiary and foreign language rights, contact info@worthymedia.com

Cover design: Christopher Tobias
Cover photography: Amy Dickerson; photo provided courtesy of Provident Label Group
Interior design: Susan Browne Design

Printed in the United States of America

11 12 13 14 15 16 /DCI/ 25 24 23 22 21 19 18 17 16 15 14 13 12 11 10 9 8 7 6 5 4 3 2 1

what i learned from

a simple blessing

THE EXTRAORDINARY
POWER OF AN
ORDINARY PRAYER

Michael W. Smith

with Thomas Williams

 **ZONDERVAN®**   A WORTHY BOOK

ZONDERVAN.com/
AUTHORTRACKER
follow your favorite authors

*Among the many blessings of my life was
Debbie's grandmother, Kate Washburn—"Nanny" to the
kids and "Kate Dear" to me! I never felt like an in-law;
she welcomed me into the family, as her own grandson,
from the very start. Of her ninety-six years, I was
privileged to know her for more than twenty-nine
years—years that she filled with love of family,
compassion for others, and commitment to the Lord.
Oh, and her one-liners were legendary!
No one was around Kate for long
without getting a taste of her humor!*

*So I lovingly dedicate this book to Nanny.
I look forward to the tremendous blessing of
being with her again, forever this time..*

Contents

Introduction 9

The Prayer of Blessing 18

1. What Does It Mean to Pray for Others? 21

2. The Prayer for Spiritual Health 43

3. The Prayer for a Pure Mind 65

4. The Prayer for Personal Holiness 89

5. The Prayer for Backyard Blessings 109

6. The Prayer for Spiritual Victory 137

Notes 163

Introduction

I HAVE BEEN BLESSED ALL MY LIFE. I'm not speaking just of the abundance of what God has given me, though those blessings are extravagant and too many to count. I mean I have been blessed verbally all my life. Godly people have actually said words of blessing to me. As far back as I can remember, my dad and mom have blessed me. Not only by being amazing, loving, and supportive parents, though they were every inch that. They blessed me with words. With encouragement. With positive reinforcement. There's no way to know how much good that did me in my growing-up years. There's no doubt that I am the man I am today because of my mom and dad.

Later, Don Finto, who was pastor of the Belmont Church in Nashville, became a greatly respected mentor to me. He often spoke a blessing over me — and he still does to this day.

These spoken blessings have been such a big part of my life that I guess it was natural for me to say blessings over others. I still do it. For example, when a member of my band was leaving rehearsal to embark on a trip, I sent him on his way with a blessing.

Fairly recently, this idea of praying blessings over people has gained an even larger importance for me. Let me tell you why.

I have toured the world for many years, giving concerts in cities from continent to continent and border to border. At each stop I meet people in all walks of life, from the rich and famous to middle-class families in the suburbs to people struggling to get by. Most of these encounters are brief and perhaps what some would call superficial. Yet I draw a lot of pleasure and meaning from them.

While I don't claim any kind of clairvoyance or special insight, I do believe that over time one learns to read certain subtleties in what people say and how they respond—subtleties that reveal an overall sense of their spiritual well-being, or lack of it. Mostly these revelations come through loud and clear in what people talk about. It shows where their minds are, or more to the point, where their hearts are.

At some point I began to notice a subtle change in the people I met. What I sensed was not anything I could put my finger on or analyze from specific data. Yet there seemed to be a shift in people's expectations about what made life good, what made it worth living. Of course, most people who come to my concerts already believe in God, are friends of believers, or are scoping out Christianity to see whether it has answers. Music can often be the key to helping these people. It can reach beyond the capacity of words and touch chords in people's hearts in ways that open them up to learning more.

What I sensed from my conversations was this: almost everyone is looking for blessings of some kind. No surprise there; we all hope to find God's blessings. But the change I sensed was in the kind of blessings they wanted. On the one hand, people were hoping God would bless them with a higher income, a lower stress level, better relationships, better child care, better transportation, even a better church with a better teacher and a better worship pastor. To the people I spoke with, these and similar things were their greatest needs.

At the same time, I was hearing more about needs of an altogether different sort—spouses cheating on each other or leaving, children on drugs, the struggles of single parents, maxed-out credit cards, bankruptcies, and addictions to drugs, alcohol, gambling, or pornography.

It didn't take long to see that the desire for blessings and the problems these people were experiencing were two heads on the same monster. The first list showed me what these people wanted, and the second showed me what they got. It wasn't hard to see that the second was often the natural result of the first. If people would change what they were pursuing, they wouldn't find themselves staring through the shattered window of broken dreams and torn relationships.

In short, it seemed to me that many of the people I encountered were simply looking for blessings in all the wrong places. It was clear that many were becoming infected by the culture that surrounds us—a me-saturated culture of instant gratification that breeds high expectations of comfort, entertainment, and material wealth.

This change disturbed me. I began to see pain in the midst of our land of plenty. And I really hurt for these people. You can't hear stories like I heard without it touching your heart—often because I have experienced a tinge of their problems myself. I felt a real need to help, to do something to address all this pain. So I made these looming human needs a part of my personal times of prayer, asking God to meet each individual in a way that only he could. Yet I had the nagging feeling that I could be doing more. It occurred to me that in some way I should be using my onstage exposure to help people address these growing concerns. But what could I do?

I remembered the power of praying a blessing. As I said above, such prayers have long blessed me, and throughout the years I have blessed others with such prayers. Maybe I could bless my concert audiences in a similar way. I could pray a prayer of blessing over them. In terms of getting God's attention, I knew that a spoken prayer in front of an audience is not likely to be any more effective than my private prayers. But I thought it might have the added power of calling people's attention to the source of blessings they might have forgotten. I decided to try it.

I wanted this blessing to be specific enough to cover many of the issues that I felt needed addressing—those growing areas of hurt that I had been witnessing. So I did a little research and found several blessings from various sources. I drew from these, wrote sections and phrases from my own heart, and added Moses' blessing from Numbers 6:24–26 at the end. The blessing has changed somewhat over time, but the prayer of blessing I generally use now is reproduced on the page following this introduction.

I first spoke this prayer of blessing to a captive audience on an Alaskan cruise ship. The response, which I will explain in the first chapter, was utterly unexpected and overwhelming. Based on this experience, I began to include the prayer of blessing at the end of many of my concerts. I still do that, and the response continues to inspire me.

As it became clear that the prayer of blessing was

touching a deep chord with people, I saw a need to explore the meaning of the prayer and address it to a wider audience. It was obvious to me that there was a broader need out there for the kind of thing my prayer was offering. That is why I decided to write this book. I want to help Christians learn what I learned from this prayer of blessing. I want to help them learn to focus on what is truly valuable and seek the only blessing that can make us truly happy: God's blessing of character.

Just so there won't be any misunderstanding, let me say emphatically, right here and now, that there is nothing "magical" about this prayer of blessing. It's not a formula to assure you of vast material blessings or even of a trouble-free Christian life. It's nothing like an incantation or a discovery of some secret buried deep in an obscure Old Testament passage that will mystically turn your life around. It is not something you can use to manipulate God into giving you whatever you want. God does not respond to words or formulas. He responds to the heart. There is no way we can use prayer or God's promise of blessing to gain what we term today as "the good life." God's real blessings are not of that sort. They are better.

Yet I am convinced that in this book you will find simple, biblical principles of living that can turn your spiritual life into something beautiful that soars above the mundane and finds the true joy that God yearns for each of us to experience. That is the blessing I pray that you will find as you read this book.

This book breaks the prayer I pray into its six specific blessings. Each chapter begins with a quote containing the segment of the blessing it will address. Then the chapter explains the value of the blessing and gives practical guidance in how to open oneself to the blessing and enjoy its benefits.

Let me remind you, as you read, that you are the son or daughter of the King. Not *a* king, but *the* King — the King of the universe. As his child, you are the heir to all he has. My fear is that we, like the prodigal son in Jesus' parable, can miss out on this enormous blessing awaiting us in trust by grasping for the immediate gratification of wealth, pleasure, comfort, and entertainment offered by the culture around us. That is the tragedy I fear may be happening to many Christians today. And that is the tragedy that can be averted if we understand the true nature of God's real blessings.

I am convinced that if you humble yourself before our Father, submit to him and his will for your life, and pray earnestly that he will bless you, you can receive a blessing far beyond what you can imagine.

That is the blessing I pray that you will find in this book.

The Prayer of Blessing

In the name of Jesus Christ,
I bless you with the promises of God,
which are "yes" and "amen."

May the Holy Spirit make you healthy
and strong in body, mind, and spirit
to move in faith and expectancy.
May God's angels be with you to
protect and keep you.

Be blessed with supernatural strength
to turn your eyes from
foolish, worthless, and evil things, and to shut out
the demeaning and the negative.
Instead may you behold the beauty of things
that God has planned for you
as you obey his Word.
May God bless your ears to hear the lovely,
the uplifting, and the encouraging.
May your mind be strong, disciplined,
balanced, and faith-filled.

May your feet walk in holiness and
your steps be ordered by the Lord.
May your hands be tender and helping,
blessing those in need.
May your heart be humble and
receptive to one another
and to the things of God, not to the world.

God's grace be upon your home,
that it may be a sanctuary of rest and renewal,
a haven of peace where sounds of joy
and laughter grace its walls,
where love and unconditional acceptance
of one another is the constant rule.

May God give you the spiritual strength to
overcome the evil one
and avoid temptation.
May God's grace be upon you to
fulfill your dreams and visions.
May goodness and mercy follow you
all the days of your long life.

CHAPTER 1

What Does It Mean to
Pray for Others?

IN THE NAME OF JESUS CHRIST,
I BLESS YOU WITH THE PROMISES OF GOD,
WHICH ARE "YES" AND "AMEN."

THE FIRST TIME I PRAYED the prayer of blessing over one of my audiences was at the evening concert on an Alaskan cruise. I had never hosted a cruise before (nor had the desire to), but I quickly warmed up to the idea after finding myself on the ship with my family, close friends, some special guests, and the large group of people who had signed up to take part.

It was a diverse cross section of folks, to say the least. There were people who were single, people who were married, and some single parents. There were a few families with children who had special needs. I got a great deal of satisfaction from the opportunity to meet them all and listen to their stories. Having spent over a week mixing with the passengers, I had learned much about their hopes, needs, and problems. Even before the cruise, I had begun to sense a growing hunger in people for blessing—a sense that the stability and moorings people had once found in their faith were slipping into confusion and even despair. The stories on this cruise were no different. It was clear to me that people needed prayers for God's blessing.

At the end of the concert, I told the audience I wanted to pray a prayer of blessing over them. As I prayed, and especially at the end of the prayer when I looked out over the audience, I sensed that it was a highly spiritual moment. How you can know in these moments that something spiritual and meaningful is happening is hard to explain. But when it happens, you know it. There's just something in the air.

And if there had been any doubt, what happened after the concert would have erased it without a trace.

HOW PEOPLE RESPOND TO BEING BLESSED

For over two years I served as a pastor for a church near Nashville. As everyone who teaches in a church setting knows, after every worship service people will shake your hand and often say, "I really enjoyed that message, Pastor," "You really blessed me today," or words to that effect. Pastors become accustomed to these routine responses. We know these responses are pretty much automatic because even when we've spent the morning talking about impending doom if the church doesn't get its act together, the same people still say, "I really enjoyed that sermon." (I always wanted to ask, "You mean you really enjoyed hearing doom pronounced over you?" But I never did.) When a person really does get something out of your sermon, you know it. The response is always much more specific, more intense, and often emotional.

Well, what usually happens after my concerts is similar to the experiences of a pastor who teaches on Sunday morning. After the show is over, several people from the audience come backstage to greet me, shake my hand, and tell me how much they enjoyed the performance. Or sometimes they say how much they liked a particular song. I don't doubt that they are sincere, and I appreciate their goodwill in telling me. But, frankly, such responses are so similar that over the years they run together. When a person is truly moved by something I do onstage, I know it. The intensity of his or her response manages to come through clearly.

After praying the prayer of blessing on the cruise ship

that night, I didn't know what kind of response to expect. In fact, I'm not sure I expected any particular response at all. I figured it would have about the same effect as the closing prayer of a church service—a signal that the event was over and people could feel free to leave in order to try to beat the crowd to the restaurant around the corner. Was I ever wrong! I was bowled over by what happened.

The next day we had scheduled an autograph session in the bookstore of the cruise ship. I often do this in my line of work, so I went in thinking it would be business as usual. It was anything but that. There were considerably more people in the line, and I could tell by their faces that something was different. Instead of the usual sea of smiles and happy expressions, many of the fans' expressions were quietly intense. Several eyes brimmed with tears. Instead of the usual bright-eyed and bouncy, "I really enjoyed the concert last night," I was often greeted with, "I can't tell you how much I appreciated that blessing." And I could tell they meant it, because it was spoken with sincerity and often with deep emotion accompanied by a story recounting some personal experience.

Typical of these responses was a woman who grabbed my hand in both of hers and said, "Your blessing meant so much to me. Especially the part about shutting out the demeaning and negative stuff and focusing on what is good and encouraging and uplifting. I've spent so much of my life wallowing in the negative that I've become a negative person. And sadly, I've passed on that way of looking at things to my teenage daughter. She has become critical and disapproving of everything in her life — especially me. Nothing pleases her. It's affected her grades, her friendships, and even driven her away from church."

The woman's voice broke and tears began to flow. She dabbed a tissue at her eyes and continued, "But your blessing last night opened my eyes to what I've been doing to her — and to myself — and showed me that it's not too late to change. As you said, I can start focusing on what is good and encouraging and lovely. I can reflect this in my responses to my daughter. And as I change, it will lead her to change." Then the woman smiled and thanked me.

I wasn't prepared to hear a personal confession like

this, but I really felt for her. As the father of five, I know how much it hurts a parent when a child is estranged from you even briefly over a little thing like forbidding him to see a movie or go to a party. I could imagine the pain of having that distance become permanent.

This kind of response was repeated several times that night — each with a different story, but all with a common theme. The prayer of blessing had opened their eyes to some truth of God that they had missed or neglected, often with troubling or disastrous results. The problems they expressed were varied — broken marriages, estranged children, lost jobs, financial hardships, health issues, sexual problems, addictions — you name it; it came out that night.

As person after person told me their hurts and regrets, I hugged them and offered some encouraging words, telling them that if they opened their hearts to God, he would certainly bless them with the blessing they needed most. God offers the gift freely. We need simply to put our arms out to receive and embrace it.

The following day, we had so many requests for copies of the blessing that I had to go back to my room, edit it to make it presentable, and ask the ship's crew to print copies for almost everyone.

Adding to my surprise, the responses were not contained to that night. They continued concert after concert and in the increased volume of e-mails I began to receive from people who had found encouragement in the prayer of blessing. It was as if the act of speaking those words was a catalyst for them to change the way they thought about their circumstances and discover the deep sense of purpose that God had for their lives. I received an e-mail from one man who said:

Dear Mr. Smith,

Thank you for the beautiful blessing you prayed over us at your recent concert. It gave me a great sense of peace while, at the same time, empowering me to continue to discover who I am as a child of God and discern all that God has planned for me—it's exciting! God has used you and your music as his instruments to speak healing and forgiveness to my heart. God's gift of this blessing, spoken by you, is a reminder not only of God's amazing love, but of the importance of caring for one another physically, emotionally, and spiritually. I understand blessing as the calling down of God's power and care upon someone so, as one child of God to another, I ask God's blessing upon you, your family, your music, and your ministry.

It was amazing to see people infused with a new sense of God's goodness and to watch it inspire them to bless others. So I began to pray this blessing over my audience at the end of each concert, and these kinds of overwhelming responses continued.

THE VALUE OF PRAYING FOR BLESSING

I began to wonder, what does it mean for the audience when I pray a blessing over them? Was the effect it had just a momentary emotional high carried over from the goose-bumpy thrill that live music can give? Or could it possibly be something deeper and more lasting?

I didn't know these people on an intimate level. I

didn't know their needs, their problems, their values, or whether their relationship with God was ocean-deep or wading-pool shallow. Yet it was clear that somehow this simple prayer of blessing touched a deep chord in many hearts. Why did they respond so positively? I didn't do anything to meet their needs in a tangible, physical sense. I didn't solve any of their problems. Didn't fix their broken marriages or mend their broken relationships, dry out their drug-addicted child or pay off their maxed-out credit cards.

So how did my prayer of blessing help them? Or did it help? Maybe it was just a string of high-sounding platitudes on a par with James's example of a superficial prayer: "Have a good day; stay warm and eat well" (James 2:16 NLT). That fear lurked somewhere in the dark corners of my mind. Did the prayer of blessing do anything more than make people feel good at the moment? My bottom-line question was this: is there any real value in praying for people you don't know, about problems you can't see, and about needs you can't meet?

As I have reflected on it since, I am convinced that this kind of prayer does have significance. We have many biblical examples of people praying for others they didn't know and for needs they couldn't meet personally. Moses prayed that God would "overlook the stubbornness of this people, their wickedness and their sin" (Deut. 9:27). The psalmist urged Israel to "pray for the peace of Jerusalem" (Ps. 122:6). The apostle Paul prayed for "grace to all who love our Lord Jesus Christ with an undying love" (Eph. 6:24). And he urged Timothy to see that "requests, prayers, intercession and thanksgiving be made for everyone" and to pray for "kings and all those in authority, that we may live peaceful and quiet lives in all godliness and holiness" (1 Tim. 2:1–2).

So if my prayer of blessing was doing some kind of good, just what was that good? People who have attended my concerts have soaked up this prayer like dry sponges, and I'm convinced that this exposes a deep need Christians are feeling today that is not being addressed. Something is missing in their walk of faith — something vital. And the responses to my prayer have given me a clue to what that something is.

Most of the stories I heard in response to my prayer of blessing told of lives lived mostly for the self. Stories of broken relationships usually revealed an insistence on having one's own way or using other people for selfish ends. Stories of addiction told how going after titillating pleasures entangled people in a web that sapped their will to escape. Stories of credit-card debt told of lives bound in chains by the materialistic desire to accumulate more and more for the self.

It's clear from such stories that a large number of Christians have fallen into the value system of the culture around us. But they are finding that the "it's all about me" approach to life is not working. The prayer of blessing simply served as a sort of wake-up call, reminding them of a truth they had mislaid somewhere along the way: true blessings come not from stuff or from satisfying the self; they come from submitting one's self to God. I can't tell you how many times the response to the prayer has been, "I have been living selfishly. I want to be unselfish."

I hate to say it, but I fear that this kind of self-centered living is even being planted in the hearts of unsuspecting Christians by some preachers who sell their listeners on the idea that if they will give more to God (which often means to their own ministry), God will pour into their lives all the material blessings they ever dreamed of having—wealth, prosperity, good health, and untroubled happiness. Giving to God, they say, is the key to the good life. Give your money to him, and in return he will pile on the blessings in the form of all the stuff you've longed for but couldn't afford.

God has indeed made promises to us, and he is always faithful to keep his word. That faithfulness is what I refer to in my prayer of blessing when I say, "I bless you with the promises of God, which are 'yes' and 'amen.'" The word *yes* is easy enough to understand. It means that God's promises are "for sure." They are something you can count on. The word *amen* means "let it be so." *Yes* and *amen* are ways of saying that God's promises are dependable and certain (2 Cor. 1:20). If you shape your life according to his timeless principles, you can be absolutely sure that a blessing will result.

THE TRUE MEANING OF BLESSING

Some believers are missing out on God's promises because they misunderstand what his real blessings are about. They don't feel blessed, because they are looking for a thorn-free rose garden blooming with all the stuff that will make their lives comfortable, prosperous, and pain-free.

Let me repeat here what I said in the introduction. The prayer I pray will not bring this kind of blessing. There is nothing magical about this prayer. It's not a formula to assure you of an abundant life or an incantation designed to manipulate God into giving you whatever you want.

God never promised us a rose garden. At least, not in this life. He did give us a perfect garden once, and we—that is, our distant grandparents Adam and Eve—messed it up. Now we must live with that mess. But God promises that if we will deal with that mess in his way and, by his grace, contend with the weeds and thorns and rust and rot, he will bless us. Not necessarily by taking all the problems away, but by shaping us into his image as we press through those problems. Even as we walk through the greatest hardships of life, we have the assurance that God will eventually lead us to that new and perfect garden we long for after we finish our term here. Jesus himself made the promise: "I go to prepare a place for you. If I go and prepare a place for you, I will come again and receive you to Myself, that where I am, there you may be also" (John 14:2–3 NASB).

This promise of perfection in the future does not mean God has no blessings for us here and now. Not by a long shot! In fact, God promises that if we uphold his truth and walk in his ways, he will give us not only that new garden in the future, but also real joy in this life now (John 10:10). What we need to learn, however, is that joy is not dependent on getting every desire met—that is, not those desires that infect us from the virus of today's me-culture.

Real joy comes when we get the *right* desire met—the desire for God himself, for a life led by the Spirit, fulfilling not our material desires but our deepest need, which is to be in a close relationship with our Creator. That is the source of true blessing. The only source.

If the prayer of blessing awakens people to this true source of real blessings, I am deeply gratified. I hope that, once awakened, people will not fall asleep again but rather take positive steps to change their approach to their journey of faith. To stop pursuing a self-oriented lifestyle. To become unselfish. To address the needs of others. I hope my prayer of blessing will inspire them to pray a similar blessing upon others.

BECOMING AN INSTRUMENT
FOR BLESSING

When people pray for blessings, I hope they will then take one more step. I hope they will become actively involved in being instruments in God's hands to bring the blessings they pray for into the lives of the people they know — family, friends, coworkers.

What does it mean to be an instrument in God's hands? Let me illustrate: I have a piano in my living room. It's one of my favorite instruments. When I'm writing a new song, I'll sit at that piano. I may jot down a few chord changes of the song on a scratch pad, adding notes and revising the melody until I think I have something worth pursuing. Then I will refine and polish the song until it's ready to play. But that song remains an inaudible thought in my head or on paper until I play it on my piano. In other words, nothing is heard until my fingers hit the keys and the hammers hit the strings. My piano turns my thoughts and emotions into sounds. These sounds flow out of the piano as music to the ears of listeners and, I hope, into their hearts. In other words, the piano incarnates my intent into something tangible that can affect others.

Jesus understood this principle. He was God the Father's instrument to convey his invisible mind and heart to his creation. Over and over in John's gospel, Jesus repeated that in everything he said or did, he was just passing on the heart and mind of God. He passed on to others what God the Father gave to him. He was the instrument, the conveyer of the blessing (John 5:19; 12:49–50; 14:10, 24, 31).

We are to bless others as Jesus did. We don't originate the blessing; God originates it, and it resounds through us just as my music resounds through the piano in my living room. Just as God's love resounded through the life of Jesus.

The importance of being God's instrument hits home with full force when we realize that when Jesus ascended to heaven, he took his body with him. This means God no longer has a body on earth through which he can bless others — except ours. We are charged with the task of being the body of Jesus in the world today. As Paul said, "Now you are the body of Christ, and each one of you is a part of it" (1 Cor. 12:27). We are to take up where Jesus left off. He now depends on us to take up the task Jesus was performing and convey God's heart and mind to others. To take the blessings God gives us and bless others with them.

Okay, I know this is not exactly an original idea. We've been singing songs about being "channels of blessing" for generations. I've written some myself over the course of my career. Songs like "Live the Life," "Give It Away," and "Open Arms" deal with the theme of being the hands and feet of Jesus to the world.

The idea of being God's instrument to bless others may not be new, but it is still valid — more than valid; it's vital. And I'm including it here because it is the only effective antidote to today's me-culture. The e-mails I receive, as well as what I see in the lives of people of faith, strongly indicate that this is true.

A LIFE OF SELFLESS GIVING

I've been blessed with the opportunity to travel the world to lead in corporate worship people from almost every culture you can imagine. Within these opportunities, there were specific moments when the sense of God's presence was so real, and the people's response so genuine, that it was too much for me to handle. After moments like these I often find myself facedown on my dressing room floor. But just as often, I find myself asking nagging questions like, "Was that as real for everybody else as it was for me?" Or, "Is what we experienced out there going to spur anyone on to developing the Spirit of Christ in their hearts, or was it just an emotional experience that made people feel better about themselves?" I am very aware that people can be involved in the Christian life purely for the mountaintop experiences.

This stands in stark contrast to people I have met who have allowed the reality of what God has done for them to so overtake them that they have dedicated their lives to the service of others. I came across them all the time while serving on the President's Council on Service and Civic Participation. If you were to write a story about these people's lives, the main plot would not be about them but about the people around them. These are people who know what it means to be an instrument.

When it comes to understanding what it means to be God's instrument, I love the prayer of St. Francis of Assisi. I can't think of a better way to end this chapter than with his thoughts:

Lord, make me an instrument of your peace.
Where there is hatred, let me sow love;
where there is injury, pardon;
where there is doubt, faith;
where there is despair, hope;
where there is darkness, light;
where there is sadness, joy.
O Divine Master,
grant that I may not so much seek to
    be consoled as to console;
to be understood, as to understand;
to be loved, as to love;

for it is in giving that we receive,

it is in pardoning that we are pardoned,

and it is in dying that we are born to eternal life.

Amen.

In this selfless kind of giving to others, St. Francis discovered the key to God's true blessings. Far from being a way to achieve success, ease, and comfort, Christianity calls us to live a life that forgets self and focuses on being God's instrument to show his love to others.

That is what I am learning from this simple prayer of blessing. And that is what I want to convey to you in the chapters that follow.

CHAPTER 2

The Prayer for
Spiritual Health

MAY THE HOLY SPIRIT MAKE YOU HEALTHY AND
STRONG IN BODY, MIND, AND SPIRIT TO MOVE
IN FAITH AND EXPECTANCY.
MAY GOD'S ANGELS BE WITH YOU
TO PROTECT AND KEEP YOU.

HAVE YOU EVER NOTICED that much of the time you spend in church, you are looking at the back of the head of the person sitting in front of you? Does that strike you as strange or make you feel uncomfortable? If it doesn't, maybe this idea will: the person who sits behind you in church spends much of the time they are there looking at the back of *your* head! (It makes you think twice about the way your hair looks on Sunday mornings, doesn't it?)

There are a few things that bug me about the way "doing church" has evolved in our culture. One of the biggest things is that in most churches it is entirely possible for people to be regular attenders and never make eye contact with the people around them. They never benefit from interpersonal relationships that provide the opportunity to both be blessed and be a blessing to others.

Too many of us come to church to find a moment of inspiration, a personal blessing, to fuel us for the week ahead. But most of the time, if we're honest with ourselves, nothing compels us toward involvement in the big picture of God's kingdom.

I wonder how many Christians think of God's blessings as private things between themselves and God. They come to church to receive from God, but they feel no duty to God or to others—no need to give anything of themselves.

That is not the way God intended for blessings to work. When he placed Adam and Eve in the Garden of Eden, he "blessed them" (Gen. 1:28). What does that mean? Well, when you look at the setup they had, it's obvious, isn't it? God gave this first couple everything they could think to ask for—and more. I'm not exaggerating when I say that no one ever had it so good. Adam and Eve are the only people ever to live on this planet who experienced absolute perfection in every way possible.

Adam and Eve themselves were perfect. Adam reflected God's design of the ideal man, and Eve was his flawless counterpart. Their relationship was perfect. They never had a spat, never got their feelings hurt, never pouted. Their love life was idyllic and fulfilling. Adam was always thoughtful, loving, and romantic, and Eve never had a headache. They never got sick, never aged. Their daily menu consisted of the most delicious foods, abundantly available simply for the taking. The climate and weather were so perfect they didn't bother to wear clothing, yet they never punctured a foot on a grass burr or scratched their skin on a thorn because burrs and thorns did not exist. They had an open-ended lease on a grand estate filled with towering trees, lush green grass, clear springs, and flowing rivers. No doubt about it, Adam and Eve had it made. They were enormously blessed.

But hold everything. When we read a little more about that Genesis blessing, we find that there were responsibilities attached: "Then God blessed them and said, 'Be fruitful and multiply. Fill the earth and govern it" (Gen. 1:28 NLT). So they were not just passive recipients of blessing; there was something Adam and Eve had to do in order to experience God's blessing. They were charged to multiply and govern.

Well now, are those tough conditions or what! Most people are eager to engage in that "be fruitful and multiply" process even without being urged. And the idea of ruling seems to appeal to just about everyone. We like to be in control, whether it's as the CEO of a big corporation or just having a space to call our own. But if all we see in these requirements attached to God's blessing is more gratification of natural desires, we may be missing their deeper meaning.

While the initial process of being fruitful and multiplying is no chore, the result of it certainly is. Raising kids brings huge responsibilities and requires painful sacrifices. And the idea of governing the earth or at least being king of some little hill appeals to our natural instincts—until we remember Jesus telling his disciples, "Whoever wants to be a leader among you must be your servant, and whoever wants to be first among you must become your slave" (Matt. 20:26–27 NLT). That dulls the glitter just a little, doesn't it?

THE BLESSING THAT BLESSES OTHERS

God's blessings involve more than just passive receiving. With every blessing that has a benefit for us, there seems to be a corresponding responsibility to others. We have a natural tendency to love the "me" part and to pretty much forget about the "others" part.

That's our big problem. The two parts of blessing are wrapped up in one package. The blessing received is not complete until we meet the requirement attached to it. And it seems that the requirement always involves a responsibility to others. The blessing blesses us not just by flowing from God into our lives, but by flowing on out of our lives to others.

As we discussed in the previous chapter, the piano in my living room doesn't take the music I put into it and bottle it up inside, cherish it, and consider it a private matter between itself and me. It doesn't get emotional and go into a religious ecstasy when I'm playing it and figure that's the end purpose of its being. The blessing is not complete until it passes through the instrument (there's that word again) and becomes music to the people who hear it. A blessing kept to one's self is no blessing at all.

Can you imagine Jesus leaving the glory of the throne room of heaven to come to earth only to run off to a mountaintop to spend his days communing privately with God in prayer and scroll reading? Can you imagine the apostle Paul after his dramatic conversion becoming a pious churchgoer, listening to the choir and sermons and then expecting God to bless him for having those tingling religious feelings by expanding his tent-making business into a multinational corporation?

No. Paul knew the drill. His attitude was not, "Now that I've had this encounter with Christ, I expect God to pour his blessings into me." It was, "Lord, open me up to pass on your blessings to others." And did Paul ever bless others! He undoubtedly wins the award as the most successful evangelist ever; through his missionary journeys and biblical writings, he spread the good news of Jesus to more people than any one person has ever reached since.

So the question is, what kind of life did Paul have as a result of his significant work for God? Paul gave us the answer in his own words:

Five times I received from the Jews the forty lashes minus one. Three times I was beaten with rods, once I was stoned, three times I was shipwrecked, I spent a night and a day in the open sea,

I have been constantly on the move. I have been in danger from rivers, in danger from bandits, in danger from my own countrymen, in danger from Gentiles; in danger in the city, in danger in the country, in danger at sea; and in danger from false brothers. I have labored and toiled and have often gone without sleep; I have known hunger and thirst and have often gone without food; I have been cold and naked. (2 Cor. 11:24–27)

I can guess what you're thinking, because it's hard for me not to think it myself: *Wow! If this is what you call blessing, I don't want any part of it.* But before we engrave that thought in our hearts, let's delve a little deeper into Paul's life. True, he seems to have had more than his share of hard knocks. Yet to read his letters, you'd think he was the happiest man who ever lived. He loved the words *joy, joyful,* and *rejoice,* using them repeatedly in his letters, often with great enthusiasm, as in this passage: "Rejoice in the Lord always. I will say it again: Rejoice!" (Phil. 4:4). In every instance he was speaking of his own joy or the joy of being in Christ that he shares with other Christians.

It pains me to say it, but there's no doubt that many Christians today have turned that idea on its head. Often the authenticity of the Christian life is judged by how richly one has been blessed with the things that make up what we call "the good life"—a nice house, new cars, a successful career, and a bulging bank account. When we see a Christian possessing all this stuff, we're likely to think, *God has really blessed him, so he must be doing something right.*

Don't get me wrong: some authentic Christians who are living truly godly lives do have this kind of material success. It's not a sin to be wealthy. God knows who can handle wealth and use it well and who cannot, and I believe it's likely that he gives or withholds accordingly. The point I'm making is that these material blessings, though God may choose to give them, are not the true measure of one's spiritual health.

The truth is, you don't know what goes on inside that person's mansion. Its teak paneling and tapestried walls could be a gilded prison infested with alienation, despair, debt, anxiety, addictions, or other ills. That's not inevitable; but it is sometimes the case.

A FALSE EXPECTATION OF BLESSING

This upside-down mind-set that expects God to shower Christians with material blessings has led many into a false expectation of what Christianity should do for them. They look to the church to help them achieve and maintain the culture's definition of the good life — to meet what are called "felt needs."

Many churches, responding like savvy businesses to the market, offer their members help in Christian living while neglecting to ground them in Christian doctrine. I've heard pastors put it this way: "People today want their religion to be practical, not theological." In other words, "Don't give me all that doctrinal stuff. Get on down to the bottom line: give me things I can use to make my everyday life better." Thus churches offer classes in areas where many of their members struggle — marriage, parenting, addiction or divorce recovery, financial management. Church often becomes an adjunct to help people meet the needs and solve the problems that arise from rejecting God's standards and living by the standards of the culture around them.

Or, in many cases, church is used simply as a respite

from the daily grind of the week. The Sunday morning worship hour provides a spiritual oasis in the desert of secularism. A sort of spiritual recharge to get people through the pressures of what's ahead. Therefore, it's important that the sermon be uplifting and the music inspiring and well performed. If the church doesn't provide worship that tingles, sermons that soothe, and the kind of lifestyle support they're seeking, the congregation does what all modern consumers do: they go shopping for another church with a product more to their liking.

Let me be quick to say here that it's right that churches have good teaching, and I'm a huge proponent of excellent music that inspires worship. These things are good and beneficial. The problem arises when a church majors on meeting the felt needs of its members instead of calling them to sacrificial service to others. In doing this they cater to—or perhaps produce—what has been called "narcissistic Christianity."

To be narcissistic is to place yourself at the center and expect all things to revolve around you. We all have to fight narcissism. It's been the scourge of humanity since

Adam and Eve fell. But to be authentically Christian is to fight that self-centered tendency and to become other-centered. This means the term *narcissistic Christianity* is really an oxymoron. The apostle Paul put it like this: "Do not think of yourself more highly than you ought, but rather think of yourself with sober judgment, in accordance with the measure of faith God has given you. . . . Be devoted to one another in brotherly love. Honor one another above yourselves" (Rom. 12:3, 10).

The call of Christ was never an invitation to a materially abundant, trouble-free life of comfort and achievement. No, it is and always has been a call to die. Jesus himself said this about as clearly as it could be said:

> If any of you wants to be my follower, you must turn from your selfish ways, take up your cross, and follow me. If you try to hang on to your life, you will lose it. But if you give up your life for my sake, you will save it. And what do you benefit if you gain the whole world but lose your own soul? Is anything worth more than your soul? (Matt. 16:24–26 NLT)

"Take up your cross," Jesus says. What does that mean? We see Christian crosses everywhere. On top of church steeples and hanging in church sanctuaries, on gravesites, book covers, bumper stickers, and posters; we decorate them and wear them as jewelry. We're so used to the cross as the symbol of Christianity that we no longer think about its original purpose as an instrument designed to inflict suffering and death.

But when Jesus told us to take up our cross, he *was* thinking of its original purpose. He meant we must die to ourselves—we must consider ourselves dead to the self-oriented instinct that makes us cling to our own ambitions, pleasures, and comfort. That means giving your life to Christ and being consistently guided by his Spirit. If this puts you in a situation where you must suffer, well, join the club. Its members include Paul, the apostles, Christ himself, and millions of Christians who have suffered since.

THE KEY TO SPIRITUAL POWER

Does this willingness to lay aside one's self even to the point of suffering mean we must say good-bye to joy?

Absolutely not. In fact, the opposite is true: it is the key to finding true joy, as the life of the apostle Paul clearly shows.

How did this often-persecuted apostle manage to be so buoyantly joyful? Let's see if we can figure it out.

In the history of his missionary journeys, we have the account of Paul and a fellow missionary named Silas being arrested for their Christian work. They were beaten and locked in stocks deep inside a prison. So what did these throbbing and bleeding guys do — question God's justice or wonder what had gone wrong in their Christian life? No, they *sang*! They were so happy to be suffering for their Lord that they couldn't help but burst into song (Acts 16:22–25). Happy because they were *suffering* for the Lord? Yes, you read that right. And no, they were not masochists.

It's no coincidence that Paul, the man most sold-out to the Lord, could also be the happiest. What was his secret? He tells us in Romans 5:3–5: "We also rejoice in our sufferings, because we know that suffering produces perseverance; perseverance, character; and character, hope. And hope does not disappoint us, because God has poured out his love into our hearts by the Holy Spirit, whom he has given us."

Paul was joyful even when he suffered for the Lord because he knew his suffering produced those traits that add up to a robustly healthy spirit. As long as God poured into him the blessings of perseverance, character, and hope, he would pass on those blessings to others by bringing to them the good news of God's salvation. That's what brought Paul such great joy.

Suffering does for our spirits what exercise does for our bodies. I don't know about you, but I don't enjoy exercise. When you do it right, it hurts. But I do it because I know it's vital to my health. Just as exercise provides resistance that strengthens our muscles, suffering provides resistance that strengthens our spiritual health, building up those muscles of perseverance, character, and hope.

I'm not suggesting that you should go out looking for persecution. I, for one, have no such plans! Life is complex enough without adding a martyr complex to the mix. But on the other hand, I've heard it said that if you aren't suffering something for Christ, maybe you should take a hard look at your Christian commitment. While suffering is not something to go out looking for, it may be a good indication of one's spiritual health.

That's why Paul and Silas sang in prison. They understood that their suffering validated their Christian commitment. In their time, Christianity was an oddity, and people who practiced it authentically, as Paul and Silas did, were cutting against the cultural grain and threatening the common assumptions of society. What inspired these two prisoners to sing was the realization, *We're suffering for Christ, so we must be doing something right.*

The core blessing that God gave Paul was the Holy Spirit, by whose power he was able to accomplish so much for God and live a life of blessing to others. It was the same blessing God gave to Adam and Eve—his Holy Spirit enabling them to accomplish God's purpose for them. Today God offers men and women that same Holy Spirit, by whose power we can accomplish the task of blessing the world with the blessings that God wants to give.

In that respect, nothing has changed since Eden. God still offers his Holy Spirit to live in the life of each Christian, enabling each of us to carry the life of God to others.

That is the only way we can enjoy spiritual health. In fact, a person without God's Holy Spirit living within is not merely unhealthy: spiritually speaking, he is dead.

PASSING ON THE BLESSINGS OF GOD

Lord of the Rings author J. R. R. Tolkien coined the term *sub-creators* to describe man's creative activity. By this he meant that we are not truly the originators of anything we create. Both our creative powers and the materials from which we create come from God. When we create anything, we merely recombine, filter, or amplify what God has given us.

In the same way, we Christians are called to be "sub-blessers." We have no original blessings to give; we merely pass on what God gives us. That's been our assignment since Adam and Eve.

If we think of ourselves merely as recipients of God's blessings and make no attempt to pass on the blessings to others, we become self-centered and do great damage to our spiritual health. Let me illustrate how this works with a personal example.

One of my favorite places is a nature reserve located just south of Nashville, called Radnor Lake. This small freshwater lake has a walking trail about three miles around. It's the kind of idyllic place that's often hard to find near urban settings: a beautiful body of water surrounded by woods jam-packed with wildlife. I go there to walk and pray when I'm faced with big decisions or just need to be alone with God.

On the southeast corner of the lake is a small pool that's cut off from the rest of the water by a paved portion of the walking path. I know when I'm coming up to it because I can smell it from about fifty yards away — it gives off a terribly putrid stink. A dark green scum covers the water, and scrubby skeletons of stunted trees and bushes protrude from its surface like groping dead claws. This pool is totally cut off from the ebb and flow that churns in the greater portion of the lake and keeps it clean.

That's what happens when fresh water stops its flow.

When a pool gathers water and fails to pass it on, it stagnates. It smells bad and becomes diseased and dead. Nothing good can live in it. Had this branch of water not been cut off from the lake by the man-made path to form a self-contained pool, it could have remained fresh and alive like the rest of the lake.

Blessings hoarded cause spiritual atrophy and death. Blessings passed on keep our lives open to be filled with new blessings.

God wants us to be continually open inwardly so he can continually pour his blessings into us. But this won't work unless we're open outwardly, pouring out to others what he pours into us. If we shut off the flow, we shut off our capacity to receive. And like that pool with no outlet that hoards the fresh water flowing into it, what we receive decays and cankers, bloating our spirits and becoming a breeding place for disease.

My hope for the prayer of blessing is that it will inspire people, including myself, to become unselfish channels of blessing. To pray for others—and not only pray for them, but also to allow the river of God's blessing to pass through our lives and outward to others.

I pray that we will be more than just ears, merely hearing and thrilling to God's music in the privacy of our spirits. I pray that we will be God's instruments, playing his music on our heartstrings so that it flows outward to bless those whose discordant lives need its healing harmonies.

CHAPTER 3

The Prayer for
a Pure Mind

Be blessed with supernatural strength to turn your eyes from foolish, worthless, and evil things, and to shut out the demeaning and the negative. Instead may you behold the beauty of things that God has planned for you as you obey his Word. May God bless your ears to hear the lovely, the uplifting, and the encouraging. May your mind be strong, disciplined, balanced, and faith-filled.

ILIKE GOING TO THE MOVIES.

I like the overly busy carpet that blares at you when you walk into the lobby of the local theater. I like playing the trivia game that runs on the big screen before the lights go down and the movie begins. I even like paying too much for popcorn with way too much butter on it. I'm a sucker for that stuff.

As much as I like the experience of being swept away in a great story, I find myself having to be increasingly selective about which movies I go to see these days. My kids are older now, but Debbie and I still try to filter out the inappropriate. I've found myself sitting in the theater halfway through a movie that I've already paid to see with a pit in my stomach over what's happening on the screen. I've felt the tension of deciding whether to get up and walk out. You'd have to be completely naive to ignore the cultural shift that's happening in the entertainment world.

For example, take the subject of heroes. My family and I got sucked into the prime-time drama *24* with everybody else. It seemed as if the entire country was hanging on Jack Bauer's every move. While Jack is, without question, the hero of that show, he doesn't reflect the purest ideals from a moral point of view. His dark side is deep and intense, full of turmoil that drives him to make impulsive decisions. Each decision leads to a cliffhanger ending that makes you crave the next episode. Perhaps it's this dark side that creates his appeal to the general public, but still, Jack doesn't represent a "true north" type of moral hero. His intentions and motives are a mix of good and evil.

To further illustrate my point, compare Jack Bauer with Christopher Reeve's Superman character in the original 1978 film. There is a vast difference between the natures of these two heroes. Superman feels squeaky clean compared to the angst of the Counter Terrorist Unit's leading man. His character represents a sense of wholesome rightness, or righteousness. There is such a stark contrast between the two that one might even refer to Jack Bauer as an antihero. Case in point: I don't have to tell my kids they can't watch Superman. Do you see the cultural progression that I'm describing?

SETTLING FOR THE NEGATIVE

This growing trend in today's entertainment troubles me because I think it's a symptom of a bigger problem. We're being conditioned to accept the negative as the normal. From time to time I've expressed to friends my disappointment with a TV show or my longing for a movie with a hero I could admire for his values or his refusal to compromise. More often than not, the response I get is that I'm not moving with the times. The movies of the past were not realistic, they tell me. They sugarcoated reality. Today's audiences don't want the syrupy stories of the past because they fail to reflect the truth. They want warts-and-all realism. They want movie heroes with real flaws like the rest of us. No one is altogether pure or altogether evil. And if movies, TV shows, and novels are honest, they will give us characters who reflect that natural mixture.

Well, I can agree with some of this. It's true that all of us are a mix of good and evil. Deep in the hearts of the best of us burrows that slimy varmint the apostle Paul calls a sin nature, "waging war against the law of my mind and making me a prisoner of the law of sin at work within my members" (Rom. 7:23).

I even agree that a movie or novel must at some level be realistic. Every good story must have a plot, and a plot involves conflict. Most of the time, this means evil of some sort must be presented. Some plots pit people against circumstances or against nature, but most of the time, stories have a villain who is motivated by evil. Still, I long to see stories of people not accepting evil as just the way things are, but fighting it—whether the evil is embedded in society, in an antagonist, or within themselves.

My complaint is not that today's films and shows are too realistic or that they show the horrors of evil. My complaint is that they do not uphold a standard of good. Presenting evil is one thing, but leading us to accept it as normal is another.

That, I believe, is where much of current entertainment is leading us—to look at certain evils as acceptable. One baby step at a time, we are being led to believe that some of the things we used to think of as evil are not really all that bad.

So the hero had to bend the law here and there to nab

the villain. If the end result is good, a few compromises along the way are justifiable.

So the hero had an extramarital affair. No one but a fundamentalist prude thinks a little sexual dalliance between consenting adults is all that bad these days.

So the hero has an alcohol problem. Oh well, we all have our flaws, don't we? Why pretend otherwise? In today's world, we can just let it all hang out because we are tolerant and nonjudgmental about what other people believe and do.

Here's the problem I see with that approach: I fear that we're being led to become morally lazy. Our affluence has given many of us almost immediate access to virtually anything we want. We have grown comfortable with indulgence, and we don't want to feel guilty about it. Guilt prods us toward the hard work of changing. That's why we want our heroes to be flawed like we are. They assure us that our weaknesses, addictions, moral lapses, and compromises are not unusual. Such heroes become mirrors reflecting a comfortable image that says, *Hey, don't get so uptight about your failures and lapses. We're all like this.*

TURNING FROM THE FOOLISH
AND WORTHLESS

It's no accident that my prayer of blessing includes the power to turn our eyes away not only from evil things but also from foolish, worthless, demeaning, and negative things. Yes, this means it's important to avoid images that present pornography, depravity, and undue graphic violence and treat moral corruption lightly. But when we center on avoiding these more obvious evils, I think we fail to see the harm done to us by overindulgence in things that are simply mindless and inane.

Maybe in our pressure-packed, overscheduled lives we need a little mindless inanity now and then. Sometimes it helps just to shift our minds into neutral for a while. But "now and then" is a far cry from the daily hours I fear many now spend as couch potatoes absorbing unreal reality shows, sitcoms that need laugh tracks to tell us they're funny, voyeuristic shows that peek into the sordid secrets of people's lives, talk shows on trivial topics, and scores of other shows that give us information we neither need, use, nor can long remember. Such fare just steals our time and leaves us with nothing useful or beneficial. And, if we're really honest with ourselves, they're not even entertaining. I suspect that we sometimes use the television as a numbing drug to slip us into a comfortable inertia that dulls realities we don't want to face.

Maybe it's a little unfair that I picked on movies and TV as ways we can waste time on "foolish and worthless things." I chose these mediums because they attract most of us — as they do me — and because I fear that much of today's mental and spiritual contamination comes through entertainment. I don't have the space to address the many other things that can draw our focus into foolish or negative arenas, but I'll briefly mention a few.

There is a tendency in pop music toward the overly sensual and profane. My involvement in the music industry over a long period of time has given me a unique perspective on this. During certain seasons of my career, I have found myself involved in what some would call the "mainstream" side of the music business, attending radio functions due to the success of singles like "Place in This World" and "I Will Be Here for You." Being in these situations as a follower of Christ was challenging. I could feel the deep battle between good and evil in the hearts and minds of those around me, as if there were some strange gravity pulling people to dwell on impure things. I feel the same struggle in popular culture today. The force of sinful human nature strains relentlessly against the desire for righteousness. We need to be on guard over what we allow our hearts and minds to dwell on.

We hardly realize how much negative mental contamination we pick up from our peers. What does most of the conversation you hear at the office consist of? Unless you work in a rare environment, most of the talk is gossip about that man in shipping who's seeing that woman in accounting on the sly. Or complaints about the callous and insensitive department manager. Or rumors about the vice president who got where he is by stealing an idea from one of his employees. Or grumbling about the long hours and low pay.

Sad to say, this kind of negativity can happen in the church as well. And sadder to say, even in the home. What should be a safe environment of love and encouragement all too often becomes a place of carping, criticism, and disrespect. The pollution of negativity sometimes seems to float in the atmosphere, and like dandelion seeds, it can take root in our lives and infest our minds before we know it. We must continually be on our guard and, more important, not contribute to the pollution ourselves.

GARBAGE IN, GARBAGE OUT

My reason for concern about what we absorb into our minds is simple. You've heard it said, "You are what you eat." We become what we fill ourselves with. The computer savvy say it like this: "Garbage in, garbage out." Fill your mind with violent images, and you're more likely to become violent. Fill it with sexual images, and you're likely to become lustful. Fill it with images of compromise, acceptance of cultural practices and values, and you're likely to adopt those values as your own. Fill it with inanity and you lose the discernment to become all God intended you to be.

Even if we believers don't adopt the culture's values overtly, we have a perverse capacity to adapt these values to our own wants. I've heard Christians say they fudge on their income taxes, but they feel justified because they don't approve of how the government wastes their money and promotes immoralities such as abortion or bans on prayer. Some Christians justify cutting corners in their businesses because it enables them to give more money to the church.

I have even heard of one executive in a faith-based company who deliberately delayed payment to suppliers because the extra interest he earned by holding the money longer was "good stewardship of God's resources." It doesn't take much imagination to wonder what this man's vendors thought of his character.

These sad facts show that it's not realistic to think we can fill our minds with corrupting images yet hang on to what we know is right. When we continually expose our minds to the standards of the culture, those standards begin to seep into our lives. The fatal change comes so gradually that, like the frog in the kettle, we don't even notice it. First we are no longer shocked by evil. Then we become accustomed to it. Then we tolerate it. Then it's only a tiny step to accept it as normal.

AVOIDING CULTURAL CONTAMINATION

To receive God's blessing and become blessers ourselves, Paul urged us to "stay away from every kind of evil" (1 Thess. 5:22 NLT). That means we must avoid the contamination of the surrounding culture. Easier said than done, Paul. How can we avoid exposure to the evils of our culture? Should we pull up stakes and move into an isolated commune with other believers or find an uninhabited island somewhere? No, Paul recognized that we must interact with all kinds of people, good and evil (1 Cor. 5:9–11). He means we must find a way to keep those evil influences from ruining our character.

So how do we keep the surrounding cultural contamination from filling our minds? Paul's answer: "Don't copy the behavior and customs of this world, but let God transform you into a new person by changing the way you think. Then you will learn to know God's will for you, which is good and pleasing and perfect" (Rom. 12:2 NLT).

Very well, Paul. I would like to have my mind transformed in this way. I would love to change the way I think so I am open to God's will. But how do I do that? The culture is all around me. It presses in on me. Every TV show has some kind of immorality. If it doesn't, the commercials do. In fact, it's everywhere I look—billboards, movies, conversations at the office, ads in the mall, business practices—I can't get away from the culture. How do I avoid its influence?

Again, Paul has the answer: "Fix your thoughts on what is true, and honorable, and right, and pure, and lovely, and admirable. Think about things that are excellent and worthy of praise" (Phil. 4:8 NLT). There's nothing mysterious about that; it's just plain and simple logic. You don't want your mind filled with contamination? Well, then, fill it with something pure. (Do we sometimes make this more complex than it really is, or what?) To fill your mind with cultural garbage leaves no room for God to pour in the blessings he wants you to enjoy.

SETTING OUR EYES ON THE POSITIVE

This need to fill our minds with things that are "excellent and worthy" is what prompted me to add the next phrase in my blessing: "May you behold the beauty of things that God has planned for you as you obey his Word. May God bless your ears to hear the lovely, the uplifting, and the encouraging."

Even though the corruption of culture surrounds us like polluted air, it is always possible to find the good that remains inherent in God's creation. We can do this because as believers we have the privilege of calling on the power of the Holy Spirit within us to resist those evil influences and hold instead to God's standard of good. Even though our sinful natures may undermine our attempts to meet that standard, we can stand strong.

We have the assurance that God's grace is sufficient for us, freeing us from the bondage of legalism. We are no longer locked up by a sense of duty; instead, we are compelled to holy living by his great love for us. Because of this grace, we are free to live our lives in a way that reflects his purity. We can refuse to lower the bar in order to justify our failure. We will never grow into the glorious creatures God knows we can be unless we keep his high standard as our goal, not the standards culture sets for what is righteous and what isn't. We can increase our capacity for obedience to God's leading by keeping our eyes and ears attuned to what is good, lovely, uplifting, encouraging, and positive.

God created us in his own image. Of course, that doesn't mean we can be God as he is; it means we can become little duplicates of him. We won't achieve the glorious potential God has in store for us if we keep our eyes lowered to the mirror of merely what is; we must lift them to the window of what can be. That's why the anti-heroes of today's entertainment can hurt us. They keep us glued to the mirror instead of the window. If we want to do more than just drift along in the cultural stream, it helps to search out models of goodness, purity, honor, character, and courage, both in our entertainment and in real life.

Why are such models helpful? Because sometimes the desire for greatness incubates better in the imagination than in the will. An inspiring example motivates us better than a sermon. Mustering up the will to reach higher seems like a lot of hard work. It means waging a serious battle with that sin nature that's sure to snarl and fight back at any attempt to muzzle it. But watching a Maximus in *Gladiator* or an Oskar Schindler in *Schindler's*

List or a William Wallace in *Braveheart* kindles our better instincts and makes us long to be grander than we are. These heroes open a window and let in a refreshing blast of clean air that inspires us with a glimpse of what we can be. The great advantage to having such heroes is that they don't badger us into changing; they inspire us to want to change.

THE BLESSING IN BITING THE BULLET

It's not easy for us to cut against the cultural grain — to turn away from what everybody about us accepts as normal. We all have a strong urge to fit in, to be accepted, to be liked. Standing against this impulse doesn't just happen; it must be intentional. It means changing long-standing TV habits, refusing to respond to certain kinds of humor, and rejecting many of the culture's assumptions. Making these changes is likely to cost you something. When a group from the office — or even from the church — invites you to join them in seeing a popular movie that you know is full of explicit sexual content or needless violence or compromised ethics, you may be scorned for declining. Peer scorn is a particularly painful form of adversity. When friends show irritation at our "puritanical attitude," it hurts. We feel excluded, shut out, isolated.

But if we maintain that standard of goodness that God has demonstrated for us, we've got to bite the bullet and make the hard decision. We are called to be different, even when it means adversity. And you can count on it: it will mean adversity, whether mild or more extreme. In this world of upside-down values, people are increasingly ridiculed or denounced for upholding Christian principles.

None of this sounds much like a blessing, does it? But it is. To see how adversity temporarily hides the best of blessings, let's look back at a classic movie almost everyone has seen — Frank Capra's *It's a Wonderful Life,* starring James Stewart and Donna Reed. Stewart plays George Bailey, a bright young man with big ambitions. George is poised to get out of the small town of Bedford Falls and make his fortune in the wider world. But the sudden death of his father leaves him stuck with the family business, a chronically struggling building-and-loan company that provides affordable housing for the town's blue-collar residents.

George has no intention of running the one-horse business for long. But various setbacks keep him from getting on with his dreams. He marries, but a panicked run on the loan company deprives him of a honeymoon. His brother, whom he expected to return and run the business, marries and moves off to the big city. George watches in frustration as others achieve their dreams while his lie buried. But he bites the bullet and sticks by his duties to the town and his growing family as he struggles to keep the business alive and make ends meet.

George's adversities come to a head when irresponsible Uncle Billy loses eight thousand dollars of the company's funds. The resulting shortfall means certain criminal charges against the innocent George.

In despair, George Bailey seriously considers killing himself so his life insurance policy will save the business and provide for his family. But the inept angel Clarence prevents the suicide by showing George the enormous ways his sacrifices have blessed people. Saving his brother from drowning resulted in his brother's saving a company of soldiers in the war. Preventing a pharmacist's mistake saved the life of a child and saved the pharmacist from becoming the town drunk. Staying in Bedford Falls and loving Mary saved her from a stunted life of loneliness and depression. And keeping open the struggling company saved Bedford Falls from the spidery web of the evil Mr. Potter, who would have reduced its inhabitants to poverty and turned the town into a pit of sleaze and corruption.

These events alone show how George Bailey's sacrifices, adversities, and choices to do the right thing resulted in enormous blessings to many people. But the cherry on the sundae comes in the last scene when the grateful town rallies around him and raises the money to save his business. That's when George realizes that his life has much more meaning than it would have if he had followed his ambitions of big-time success. Surrounded by his loving family and a multitude of grateful friends, he realizes that he is the richest man in town.

Heroes with strong character like George Bailey inspire us to swim against the current of the mainstream and become the exceptional creatures God intended. People like George paint a powerful picture of what we can be if we direct our eyes, ears, and hearts away from the demeaning and negative and toward the uplifting, encouraging, and beautiful. Toward the blessings God wants to shower on us.

THE TRUTH ABOUT REALITY

I know that today's movie critics would dismiss films such as *It's a Wonderful Life* as unrealistic, wishful fantasies with impossibly good heroes and sappy happy-ever-after endings. As I noted earlier, such movies are accused of giving us a false picture of life, not life as it really is.

I beg to differ. The grunge, corruption, immorality, and violence that critics like to call reality are not reality at all. They are blights on reality, as rust is a blight on metal, mold is a blight on food, and pond scum is a blight on water. The true reality is found beneath the blight in what God created in the beginning—the perfection of the world as he originally made it. Only the good that God created is real. We came along and added the corruption, evil, pain, decay, and death, which are not reality but contaminations of reality.

To make the concept clearer, if you leave a hammer outside in the weather long enough, you will find its head completely covered with rust. None of the original metal will be visible. If you value the hammer, you will not accept the rust as its true reality. The true reality is the metal beneath the rust. You will use oils and abrasives to clean away the rust and restore the hammer to its original condition — its true reality.

That's how God looks at the world. He created it pure and uncontaminated. Our original ancestors misused it, and the result is the rust of death, pain, grief, and all the troubles we deal with now. But God values his creation, and he fully intends to remove the rust and restore everything to its original uncontaminated perfection.

That is the ultimate reality. That is true realism. The ugly stuff we contend with day by day is the rust. The stuff we see portrayed in TV and films and other forms of entertainment mistakenly treats the rust as the reality. So when we choose to set our eyes and ears on purer things, when we learn to prefer real heroes and happy endings, we are showing our commitment to the true reality that God has promised. The story God wrote has a happy-ever-after ending that promises eternal joy to those who focus on the pure and lovely and adopt true character into their lives. If we focus our eyes and ears on things that give us glimpses of that happy reality, it will go a long way toward enabling us to receive the blessings God wants to pour into us.

That is why I pray so fervently that you and I will commit ourselves to turning away from the foolish, worthless, evil, demeaning, and negative things the culture thrusts at us. I pray that we will focus instead on the lovely, the uplifting, and the encouraging. That's where we find true blessing. And that's how we can become blessings to others who need models to show them the truth they so desperately need to know.

CHAPTER 4

The Prayer for
Personal Holiness

MAY YOUR FEET WALK IN HOLINESS AND YOUR STEPS BE
ORDERED BY THE LORD. MAY YOUR HANDS BE TENDER
AND HELPING, BLESSING THOSE IN NEED. MAY YOUR
HEART BE HUMBLE AND RECEPTIVE TO ONE ANOTHER
AND TO THE THINGS OF GOD, NOT TO THE WORLD.

WHEN IT CAME TO HOLINESS, no one could hold a candle to Sister Agatha. In the minds of those who knew her, she was holiness personified. She attended church regularly, read her Bible daily, spent hours every day on her knees in prayer and meditation, fasted once a week, didn't have a TV in her home, shunned jewelry and makeup as worldly, and urged others in the church to follow her example. She monitored the preacher for scriptural accuracy and did him the favor of pointing out his misstatements. She claimed that a drop of liquor had never crossed her lips and a curse word had never escaped them. When reminded that Jesus himself drank wine, she replied, "I know. And I didn't think any better of him for it." As someone said of Sister Agatha, "She's as holy as Swiss cheese."

Sister Agatha is not actually a real person, but she embodies what my idea of being holy was like when I was very young. I thought being holy was all about praying, meditating, fasting, Bible reading, abstaining from worldliness, and doing churchy stuff. When certain Christians were spoken of as being holy, it was not always meant as a compliment. And it's still not.

I'm sure you've heard the term *holier than thou* applied to some who seem to look down on others who lack their high spiritual attainments. Churches that express more enthusiasm in worship than we're comfortable with are often called "holiness" churches, and their members are sometimes unkindly referred to as "holy rollers." Of course, it's possible that these negative terms are thrown at them unfairly because their commitment makes less dedicated believers look bad.

Partly because of these misguided attitudes and expressions, somewhere along the way I picked up some wrongheaded ideas about holiness. I had the idea that to be holy means to have one's head in the clouds. To be otherworldly. To live a life largely defined by rules and restrictions and don'ts—don't smoke, don't drink, don't cuss, don't chew, and don't associate with people who do. Even when I began to grow out of these false impressions, I still thought of holy people as those who carried around an aura of highly developed religious refinement. They were churchgoers, Bible readers, fasters and prayers, and maybe just a little too heavenly to be of any earthly use.

Today I know better. Being holy certainly doesn't mean what I once thought it meant. When I include in my prayer of blessing a desire that people will walk in holiness, I'm simply praying that they will be receptive to the things of God instead of to the things of the world. I am praying that they will be holy. But the holiness I pray for has very little to do with what I once thought it did.

THE TRUTH ABOUT HOLINESS

The simplest definition of *holy* is "being like God." That may involve a few or several of the practices I mentioned above, but none of them is the essence of holiness. If we want to be holy, we will pattern our lives after God as closely as possible. And just how do we do that? We have a perfect model: Jesus was *Emmanuel*—God with us. In the Gospels we can look at him at any time, whatever he is doing, and see exactly what God is like. In Jesus we see holiness in its purest form.

What do we see when we look at Jesus? How did he

demonstrate holiness? Maybe the best answer is the one he gave to John the Baptist when John sent a message from his prison cell, questioning whether Jesus was the One they had been expecting God to send. To confirm that he was God's Holy One, Jesus did not send back the answer we might expect: "Tell John that I pray five times a day, fast three times a week, never eat without going through ritual purification, never miss a synagogue meeting, burn the midnight oil studying the holy scrolls, avoid everything unclean, and wouldn't touch a drop of wine even with gloves on." Instead, he responded, "Go back to John and tell him what you have heard and seen — the blind see, the lame walk, the lepers are cured, the deaf hear, the dead are raised to life, and the Good News is being preached to the poor" (Matt. 11:4–5 NLT).

Here Jesus shows us clearly that being holy does not mean wearing a suit and taking a Bible to church. It doesn't mean praying long, eloquent prayers; fasting like a weight-watcher; saying "praise the Lord" a lot; or holding up your hands in church. It means getting those hands involved in God's work. Getting them dirty. Being holy means feeding the hungry, seeing to the needs of the sick, helping people in trouble, and comforting them in grief. It means letting your hands be instruments of God's love. It means opening your life to God's Holy Spirit and allowing him to use you to bless others.

One of the best examples of holiness is Mother Teresa. She wasn't holy because she dressed in a starchy black nun's habit and lived a cloistered life of prayer and meditation. She was holy because she dedicated her life to ministering through hands-on, physical contact to the most shunned, ostracized, and repugnant people on earth — the lepers in the filth of Calcutta's slums.

I have seen similar examples of holiness firsthand. I was in Haiti in the aftermath of the January 2010 earthquake, and I'll never forget seeing teams of Samaritan's Purse volunteers meeting the needs of the devastated and demoralized around them out of the fullness of Christ's love within them. Or meeting the Haitian pastor who showed me his house that had crumbled under a five-story school building, killing his wife, baby, mother, and mother-in-law. Amid his unbearable grief was a deep commitment to reflect the reality of God's goodness in the chaos around him. I was so overtaken by the generosity I observed in those serving around me that I was inspired to lend a hand where I could, serving at feeding stations and providing moments of distraction for kids by playing with and praying for them. Even in the epicenter of tragedy, hope was contagious.

These dedicated Christians blessed others deeply. And they did it at considerable sacrifice to themselves. They did not get paid for their work. Some may have been supported by churches or donations, but many had no financial support and even paid their own travel expenses. Some of them lost salaries or shut down their own businesses for a time in order to bless others. Some were injured or came down with diseases in the course of their service.

BEING HOLY AND HELPING OTHERS

It's no coincidence that in my prayer of blessing I connect holiness with having hands that are "tender and helping, blessing those in need." The Bible shows us in many places that God connects holiness—being like him—with the way we care for others and meet their needs. Christ's answer to John quoted a few pages back is one example. Another is in John the apostle's letter, where he wrote, "For anyone who does not love his brother, whom he has seen, cannot love God, whom he has not seen. And he has given us this command: Whoever loves God must also love his brother" (1 John 4:20–21).

It's significant that when Jesus spoke to his disciples of final judgment, the criteria he used to separate the saved people from the lost was whether they had fed the hungry and thirsty, given shelter and clothes to the needy, looked after the sick, and comforted those in trouble with the authorities (Matt. 25:31–46). The people who did these unselfish deeds for others were the ones who were holy, the ones who were most like God.

I'm not trying to weigh you down with some sort of works-based theology here. If there's one thing I know, it's that there's nothing we can do to justify ourselves in the presence of a holy God. The apostle Paul makes that clear in his letter to the church in Ephesus: "For by grace you have been saved through faith. And this is not your own doing; it is the gift of God, not a result of works, so that no one may boast" (Eph. 2:8–9 ESV). But there is an undeniable relationship between faith and good works. One will lead to another. A vibrant and healthy faith will produce good works as surely as an apple tree will produce apples. They just go together. James puts it this way: "For as the body apart from the spirit is dead, so also faith apart from works is dead" (James 2:26 ESV).

Why does God put so much stress on our love for him being expressed through service to others? I think the answer is pretty simple. As the apostle John tells us, God is love (1 John 4:16). That's what he's about. God created us out of love, and he loves us in many ways — as an artist loves his painting, as a musician loves his song, as a father loves his child, and in a vivid image used over and over in the Bible, as a lover loves his beloved. Love is what God is all about.

When our first parents rejected God in Eden, he was heartbroken. But he honored their choice and stepped out of their lives, grieving at the separation and the pain and suffering their choice would bring to their race. In spite of this rejection of his love, God sent his Son to show his love, not only in the great sacrifice to atone for our sins but also to demonstrate his love hands-on by serving and ministering to the hurts and needs of those he encountered while he was here.

After Jesus returned to heaven to prepare for our coming, he gave us the high honor of being his body on earth. We are to be channels through which God's love flows to others. We allow him to use our hands and our hearts to provide the blessings he wants to give to those who hurt and grieve. That's what being like God means. That's being holy.

TODAY'S CRYING NEEDS

I don't have to tell you that opportunities for showing this kind of love are thrust at us everywhere we look. The world around us groans with hurt that desperately needs the healing touch of God's love. Wherever I go, I meet people who are distraught for many reasons — broken marriages, children who have gone wrong, financial hardships, health problems, job losses, or out-of-control addictions. I've met people who can see nothing positive in their lives, either in the present or the future. I meet people whose lives seem good on the surface, but beneath the cool exterior boils a cauldron of pain, anguish, uncertainty, and a sense of meaninglessness that may have no source they can put their finger on. I've seen people who live under a continual curse of negativity. Many have been raised by negative parents or, for a growing number, by an abusive parent or a single parent disillusioned and stressed out by the challenge. Raised in such an environment, many grow up viewing life through a smudged and shattered lens.

Many who are raised in such an atmosphere saturated with negativity and pain find themselves unable to experience God's blessings. Their lives are so full of pain that there is no room to receive the healing love God wants to give, and thus they are trapped in a cycle of negativity, passing on to others the pain they live with.

The surprising thing about all this hurt is that it seems such a paradox. Is it just me or does it seem to you that in this immensely blessed country of unparalleled affluence, unlimited opportunity, and unrestricted worship, we are seeing more shattered lives, more disillusionment, more loss of faith, more emptiness, more loneliness, more lack of direction than seems reasonable to expect? It's a time when the opportunity is wide open for us to see this despair and bless hurting lives by being there and showing them the love of God. We can model to them a better way of living and responding to negative influences.

It pains me to say it, but I see many believers today who are unable to be the blessing they want to be because they are feeling the same despair as the rest of our culture. How can this be? I think it's largely because so many have been caught up in our society's concept of what blessing means. As a result, they are reaping the same despair as their neighbors.

In our country today, we are conditioned to think of blessings largely as wealth, ease, success, and pleasure. We can hardly blame those who fall into this snare because, as I mentioned earlier, there's a swarm of preachers out there contributing to this misguided way of thinking. Many do it deliberately by preaching that if you give your life to God (and your money to their ministry), God will bless you with all kinds of material wealth. Others teach this message more subtly. One church recently drew an Easter crowd by advertising a new car giveaway for the winner of their Easter lottery. The only requirement for a ticket was to attend the Easter service.

It's probable that the church leaders who planned this event did it with pure motives. Knowing how hard it is to get nonmembers into a church, maybe they figured, "If we can just get visitors in the door, we can give them the true message of Christ." But I fear they may have given the public an unwitting affirmation of material desires and signaled the church's willingness to cater to them.

They could even claim biblical justification for their giveaway. The Old Testament sometimes speaks of blessings in terms of material wealth. This makes sense when you consider the time. In that ancient rural economy, life and death depended on the fertility of livestock, land, and marriages. Abundance in these areas was a huge blessing because it meant survival.

But material things are not the primary blessing God has in mind for us. He's more interested in our character than our car. In this fallen world, character is seldom if ever built through having it all. That's why the New Testament often speaks of blessing in terms of character built through sacrifice and adversity.

HOLINESS, SACRIFICE, AND ADVERSITY

Adversity comes in many forms. As I noted in the previous chapter, it can be ridicule or denouncement by your peers. Or it can be danger, hardship, and financial loss suffered willingly by people like those I saw in Haiti who dedicated themselves to being God's hands.

At the point of sacrifice or adversity is where we are easily tempted to start backtracking. But that would be a mistake, because these uncomfortable challenges are usually required in the authentic Christian life. Sacrifice and adversity don't often come to us in extreme forms today, but some of it is almost always necessary as the raw material from which God builds character in us.

My guess is that you have, at times, unwittingly prayed for adversity. Think about it. What are you asking for when you pray for patience? You are probably asking for a trying situation that will demand that you be patient. What are you asking for when you pray for humility? It's likely you are asking for your ego to be brought down a few notches. What are you asking for when you pray for more reliance on God? Well, you may be asking for

God to take away those things you rely on instead of him. When you pray for God's blessings, you are praying for the kind of character that will desire to be holy and do what it takes to get there. Whether you realize it or not, you may be praying for some form of adversity that God will use like an obstacle course to condition you into a strong and fit soldier for his service.

I suppose the natural tendency on discovering this fact is to ratchet down our prayers a bit to avoid the adversity. But deep down in your heart, is that really what you want? When you read books or watch movies featuring those heroes we mentioned in the previous chapter, don't you feel a stirring somewhere deep inside that says, "I want to be like that. I don't want to just go with the flow. I want the exhilaration of feeling the wind in my face. I want the joy that one can feel from rowing upstream when everyone else is drifting downward. I want to feel the Spirit of God with power in my life, partnering with me to be the glorious creature God created me to be"?

Jesus' parable of the talents in Matthew 25 tells of a businessman who was going on a long journey. He entrusted to three of his subordinates large sums of money: to the first man five talents, to the second two talents, and to the third one talent. In their boss's absence, the first two men took the risk of investing the money, and their courage paid off. Both doubled the investment. The third man, wanting to be safe, hid the talent entrusted to him.

On his return, the businessman highly commended the first two men, saying to each, "Well done, good and faithful servant! You have been faithful with a few things; I will put you in charge of many things. Come and share your master's happiness!" (Matt. 25:23). When the third man returned his talent to his boss intact, the businessman was livid at the waste. He threw the man out for his failure to use well what had been entrusted to him.

God has given to each of us certain abilities. These are wonderful gifts meant to be developed and used to further God's intent on the earth. This means distributing his blessings to others, spreading his love to those who need it. He has given each of us something we can use in this process. Instead of ratcheting down your prayers to avoid sacrifice and adversity, wouldn't it be better to ratchet them up in order to achieve what God would have us achieve? This is how we develop Christlike character.

Take some time to search your soul and see if you don't long to have the kind of character that will joyfully take the risk of investing what God has given to you. This is the kind of holiness that will cause God to smile at you and say, "Well done, good and faithful servant."

That's what I long to hear. That is why when I pray my prayer of blessing, I am praying for myself as well as others. I want to hear those dear words from Jesus. And I know I will never hear them if I take the safe and easy route of no risk. If I avoid the contamination of the slum or the sickbed, the distressed cry of the homeless, the hungry, or the devastated; if I ignore the pain and despair of my neighbor, I may lead an easier, safer, and less harried life, but I will miss out on enormous blessings that God longs to give me. One of the best lessons I've learned is that the act of blessing others boomerangs back to the blesser. Blessing others becomes its own blessing.

I want evil cleaned out of my life and replaced with true holiness so that I will become a vessel through which God's blessings can pour freely to those around me. I want to be an example to them. An example of one who is not caught in the downward drift of culture. One who forces selfishness out of his life by replacing it with God's love and service to others. One who changes his focus from inward to outward. One who is devoted to being holy as God is holy.

CHAPTER 5

The Prayer for
Backyard Blessings

GOD'S GRACE BE UPON YOUR HOME,

THAT IT MAY BE A SANCTUARY OF REST AND RENEWAL,

A HAVEN OF PEACE WHERE SOUNDS OF JOY

AND LAUGHTER GRACE ITS WALLS,

WHERE LOVE AND UNCONDITIONAL ACCEPTANCE

OF ONE ANOTHER IS THE CONSTANT RULE.

A FEW YEARS AGO, I was in Budapest, Hungary, playing a concert. It was the first time I had ever been in that part of the world, let alone been there to play music. No one, including the promoters of the event, knew exactly what to expect. They had exercised a great deal of faith in bringing my team and me there. We all waited anxiously to see what the outcome of the evening would be. Did anybody in Budapest know of Michael W. Smith? If they did, would they want to come see him play? We had a big room and a big sound system. It would be a shame to go through the hassle of setting all of that up if no one was going to come.

As the time of the concert grew closer, we were overwhelmed with the response. People flooded into the convention center where the event was being held. Thousands of young people pressed toward the front of the general admission "standing room only" section at the front of the stage. The atmosphere in the room was electric. The lights went black. But even in the darkness of the room, the crowd could see my band mates taking their respective positions. The crowd responded with increasing volume. I remember walking onstage as the band began to play. I was confronted with a crowd of people whose ecstatic response could only be properly understood when one realized that the reign of communism wouldn't have allowed what we were experiencing to take place twenty years prior. What a moment. People were singing every word to every song—in English! I remember the goose bumps I had on my arms while listening to their beautiful eastern European accents singing:

Holy, Holy
Are you, Lord God Almighty
Worthy is the Lamb[1]

I would be one of the most ungrateful wretches on earth if I did not thank God profusely and give him all the praise for moments like this. God has allowed me to combine my personal passion of music with my passion to praise him in a way that has blessed others. I consider myself nothing more than a teacher, and I say that with the utmost humility. Preachers teach from their pulpits, Sunday school teachers in their classrooms, and I teach through my music, as Paul urged the early Christians to do with "psalms, hymns and spiritual songs" (Col. 3:16). I am deeply grateful, and I praise God and thank him every day for these tremendous blessings. Even after more than twenty-five years in music, I have to pinch myself to be sure it's all real.

As much as I love music, and as much as I love passing on this blessing that God has poured into me, he has given me other blessings so great they make my music career seem like a bauble. And the surprising thing about these greater blessings is that I didn't have to go far to find them. Unlike my musical career, which I had to work and strive for, these greater blessings were right in my own backyard.

You see, while inclination to music was God's gift to me, it was up to me to develop that gift. (Remember the parable of the talents?) Like most artists, musicians, and songwriters, I spent untold hours learning, practicing, and knocking on doors. Meanwhile I kept starvation at bay by waiting tables, working for a soft-drink bottler, and planting shrubs for a landscaping company.

I was playing keyboard for another group when I signed my first songwriting contract with a publishing company in Nashville. I thought I had arrived in the promised land. I had all I could ask for and more. But as I was about to learn, an even greater blessing was waiting just around the corner. Or maybe I should say, just outside my door.

What was this greater blessing? I was hoping you would ask.

MY GREATEST BLESSING

I was sitting in my office one afternoon when I happened to look up and see a young woman walk by. My jaw dropped to the floor. She was the most beautiful girl I had ever laid eyes on. I fell instantly in love. When I recovered my senses, I fumbled for the phone and called my mother in West Virginia.

"Hi, Mom. I just thought you'd want to know that I just saw the girl I'm going to marry."

"Really? Who is she?" It should have occurred to me that Mom would want to know that.

"Well, I don't know," I replied. "I haven't met her yet."

My poor mother! After all she and Dad had taught me about not being swayed by a girl's good looks, being sure about her character, taking time to get to know your potential wife, and building a relationship carefully from the ground up before making a decision, she must have thought I was totally out of my head. But I had never been so clearheaded in all my life. Somehow I just knew. It was a God thing.

I hung up the phone, jumped up from my chair, and rushed into the building on a search-and-capture mission. After going through all the offices, I learned that this girl worked in the warehouse. I went to the warehouse and found that she had gone to the restroom. So I stood guard outside the restroom door to make sure nobody would get to her before I did.

When she walked out, I was wowed. She was even more beautiful up close than in that moment when she breezed by my door. I stammered an introduction and learned that she was Deborah Kay Davis. Four nights later, I took her out for the first time. Three and a half weeks later we were engaged, and four months after that we were married.

Debbie was the most unbelievable blessing God ever gave me. And after twenty-nine years of marriage, she still is. The way that I felt when I first saw her is the same way I feel about her today.

But I must be honest with you. Even if you are deeply in love, even if you have married your true soul mate, even if your marriage is made in heaven, it has to be lived out right here on the nitty-gritty earth. Even the best of marriages involve the blending of separate and sometimes opposite expectations.

Debbie and I discovered this quickly during our first year of marriage. We didn't know how different we were until we both got under one roof. We had to compromise on all kinds of issues—not the least of which was our differing sleep schedules. I was a night owl, and since my most creative hours were usually somewhere between 10 p.m. and 2 a.m., I liked nothing better than to sit at my keyboard and write during the "late shift." Deb was at her best a little earlier than that. She was basically unconscious by 10:30 p.m. and up by 7 a.m. As any musician would agree, 7 a.m. is not an ideal wake-up time. The idea of waking up somewhere in the double-digit range was much more appealing to me!

Dealing with this difference obviously required the exercise of a little flexibility on the part of both of us. Debbie was fine with me writing after dinner. In fact, she often joined me at the keyboard, and some of the songs we wrote together flowed from these times . . . candles lit, Bible open. It was a sweet beginning for our marriage.

The problem came when she went to bed in the next room, and I kept playing. Our walls were paper-thin, and even when I turned the keyboard way down, she would complain. How was I to know I would marry a girl with sensitive hearing? She tried earplugs, which didn't help. So I tried wearing headphones, which I felt sure would solve the issue. Good intentions and a great idea, but I couldn't play without stomping my left foot in rhythm. She would often appear at the door, bleary-eyed, asking if I could refrain from shaking the entire house.

Eventually, we found a happy medium. She began adjusting to staying up later, especially after she went out to sell merchandise on two of Amy Grant's tours. Nothing like the road life to change your body clock! And after our babies started coming, any illusions about maintaining our own sleeping schedules were quickly banished to oblivion.

Marriage involves the merging of two independent personalities—of their hopes, dreams, and desires. None of that just happens. The love may be strong and passionate, but love does not conquer all. To make love endure through a lifetime takes work and sacrifice. Paul may have been a single man, but he spoke with God's inspired wisdom when he wrote, "Husbands, love your wives, just as Christ loved the church *and gave himself up for her*" (Eph. 5:25; emphasis added). Yep. It's true. Even in the field of love, that persistent idea of sacrifice rears its head again. When you get married, there's a little something you have to give up: *yourself.*

Debbie was an incredible blessing, but as I learned (remember the principle we noted in chapter 2), with every blessing comes a duty. And in our fallen world, duty usually means sacrifice. Along with the blessing of a loving wife came the duty of caring for her and the

sacrifices involved in blending two independent personalities into one. That need for sacrifice often surprises
head-in-the-clouds lovers who think romantic feelings
alone will carry them through. Duty and sacrifice are the
overlooked fine print in the contract.

MY OTHER GREATEST BLESSINGS

Debbie and I both wanted a big family, and from the
moment we said "I do," we dreamed of a house filled
with the pattering of little feet. But we knew that there
was a major roadblock standing in the way of that dream.
According to her doctor, Debbie's long and serious bout
with anorexia in her teen years had left her infertile.
Though the reality of Deb's condition was devastating, we
chose to have faith for God's best, believing that he knew
our desires and would work on our behalf. We hoped for
healing. We talked about the possibility of adoption. No
matter what, we knew we loved kids and were looking
forward to being parents.

There was another option in Nashville in the early
1980s. Vanderbilt Hospital had a new fertility clinic. We

considered going, cringing at the thought of what that kind of intervention would cost. Especially since our bare-bones health insurance wouldn't cover the treatments.

One Sunday, before we set up the first appointment, we talked to our pastor. He had a simple suggestion: why not give God a chance and ask him directly and specifically for Deb's healing? He encouraged us to follow James 5:14 and come to the next elders' meeting for prayer. That meeting was a turning point in our lives. As the elders gathered around us, anointing our heads with oil and laying hands on us, their powerful prayers filled the room. We slowly got back on our feet, a little shakily. Having both experienced the same extraordinary feeling, we walked out and said to each other, "What just happened? I've never felt shock waves go through my body like that!" What had happened was that Deb's body had been healed. In about five months, we were expecting our first child. Ten years later, when we discovered that number five was on the way, I called Pastor Don and jokingly asked if he would take us off the prayer list!

I never dreamed of what enormous blessings children are. I remember the first time I held my firstborn, Ryan

Whitaker Smith. The joy and love I felt is indescribable. Holding him also drove out a secret fear that had lurked in my mind. In spite of my desire for children, I was afraid Debbie filled my heart so completely that it would be hard to find room to love anyone else. The blessing was that Ryan did not crowd out or diminish my love for Debbie one iota. Instead he doubled my heart's capacity for love. This capacity expanded four more times as Whitney, Tyler, Anna, and Emily were born. Each birth drew me closer to God, not only in deep gratitude and praise, but also because each time, my heart grew large enough to enfold another life in a bond of love. And I knew that the more God enables us to love, the more we become like him.

THE BLESSINGS OF DUTY AND SACRIFICE

I didn't realize it at the time, but somewhere along the way I learned that another blessing came to me along with having kids. That blessing took the form of dirty diapers, walking the floor at night, kids throwing up and running fevers, causing worry and requiring discipline, teaching, and training. No, the sentence you just read is not an editor's oversight. When I said in the second chapter that blessings are almost always accompanied by duties, I didn't tell you that these duties actually become blessings in themselves. Let me explain.

Born as we are into a fallen race of sinners, we all tend to be selfish. We want things our way. We want what we want when we want it. Good parents do their best to train and discipline that selfishness out of us, and good teachers and pastors reinforce the lesson. But that self-centered tendency is deep-rooted, and it almost always requires hand-to-hand combat in the arena of life where the wants of self are pitted against the needs of others. Marriage and family provides this arena. Family is the perfect challenge to selfishness. Living in a family demands that I be sensitive to the needs of others. It demands my time. It intrudes on my wants. It tramples my ego. It virtually obliterates the concept of leisure. What a blessing!

No, I'm not being facetious; these duties are truly blessings. Without such duties, we would become utterly self-centered, egotistical, and narcissistic—all of which are deadly because focus on self alienates us from God. Facing up to our duties beats down selfishness and forms godly character by challenging the supremacy of self.

Let me be quick to say that marriage and family are not the only means of beating down the curse of selfishness. Many single people and childless couples are truly godly in character, compassionate, loving, and unselfish in all their doings. But I think marriage and family provide a rewarding means of dealing with selfishness because the glue that holds us to it when we'd rather bail out is love.

Had love not held us together, either Debbie or I could've bailed out of the marriage or abandoned our family when the demands on self became too great. But we found—as all committed couples do—that if you hang in there, dedicate yourself to your family's welfare, and stick to it when you'd rather hit the road, having a family is one of the most character-forming experiences of all.

And the most rewarding.

Hiding within all the pain and frustration that comes with family are some of the most enormous blessings

God ever gives. Out of family emerges more joy than anyone deserves.

Last year as my family gathered around our dining room table on Father's Day, I paused a moment and just listened to the love. It was expressed in amiable conversation, jokes, and laughter. And I thought, *What I have here is a far better blessing than all the Grammy Awards I could ever win.* And I really meant it. I am doubly blessed that all my children and grandchildren live nearby. We share meals as often as three times a week.

I am triply blessed in that I live in a family that truly loves being together. My daughters Anna and Emily would admit, without hesitation, that they are the best of friends. How crazy is that!

I know of many families who are not together. For some, it's because of distance. For others it's by choice. I know families in which every get-together involves sadness, conflict, and heartbreak. When family relationships go sour, something vital is stolen from life. When things at home are not good, nothing seems good.

My point in all this is to say that dealing effectively with adversity is what makes family love and togetherness possible. If parents are not willing to face the adversity of sacrifice that comes with growing a marriage and raising a family, they cannot expect to reap the blessing of joy that only family can bring. Parents who try to escape the adversity by not making those sacrifices tend to end up with families that reflect the same kind of selfishness. When each is out to protect himself or herself from sacrifice, family members tend to find themselves at constant odds with other members whose very proximity and varying needs and wants intrude on their own.

After twenty-nine years of marriage and family, I tell you this with all sincerity: if it came down to a choice between family and music, believe me, I would choose family in a heartbeat. Because family is what makes my heart beat.

THE BIGGEST OBSTACLE
TO BLESSINGS

One thing that really breaks my heart—and it's one of the reasons I wanted to write this book—is that everywhere I go I find so many people for whom marriage is far from being a source of joy. In fact, it is their main source of pain, sadness, and disillusionment. I hear of people living in misery because of loveless or abusive marriages. I hear of unfaithfulness, alcoholism, addiction, neglect, and emotional bullying. More often I hear of separations, abandonment, divorce, custody battles, alimony, and child-support neglect. I hear of single parents struggling desperately to keep things together. In almost every case there is anger, bitterness, disillusionment, or despair. Tell these people that marriage is a source of joy and they'll laugh in your face.

I know it's a hard thing to say, but I must say it: in almost every instance of a miserable or broken marriage, the root cause is selfishness. Don't get me wrong; I'm not judging or accusing. But I've seen situations where both parties were so ingrained in their own sense of entitlement that it made compromise nearly impossible. I've also seen this play out in a more one-sided fashion, as individuals in marriages become so preoccupied with their own needs that they completely alienate their spouse. It seems a bit unfair in today's world to pin the blame for self-centeredness solely on the individual when it seems that society as a whole has bent over backward to push us into self-asser-tiveness, self-actualization, self-esteem, self-determination, self-reliance, self-this and self-that. The total emphasis is on independence, rights, and expectations.

Self-sacrifice gets no press these days. In fact, we are encouraged against becoming "doormats," implying that sacrifice and giving will mean the loss of selfhood and personal happiness. That's why many couples mar-rying today have lawyers write up prenuptial contracts outlining marital expectations and property distribu-tion, should divorce occur. When couples enter marriage with such demands, they miss out on the blessings that can come only from sacrificial love. They become open only to the getting and closed off from the giving. The bottled-up selfishness festers into discontent, which usu-ally ruptures and destroys the marriage. With today's pervasive emphasis on meeting the demands of self, it's little mystery why the American divorce rate hovers at 50 percent.

In such a toxic environment, it's perfectly natural to think, *But if I follow the path of sacrifice and give up the things I've wanted and dreamed of for my life, how can I be happy?* Good question. On the surface it doesn't seem to make sense. It's one of those things we won't know until we try it. It's called stepping out in faith. Jesus himself assured us that giving up our lives is the only way to have life. "If you cling to your life, you will lose it; but if you give up your life for me, you will find it" (Matt. 10:39 NLT).

The more you think about that topsy-turvy statement, the more you can see the sense of it. The big emphasis today is on enjoying ourselves. But as someone once said, "Sooner or later we find that there is nothing left in the self to enjoy."

When unopened to others, the self is a closed prison. Locked inside that prison, we become dependent on our own resources for happiness, fulfillment, and meaning. But our own resources are limited. Once we fill ourselves by satisfying our wants, that hoard of gratification becomes our total supply of resources for enjoyment. And gratification of selfish desires always wears thin and becomes tiresome.

It's only when we open ourselves outward in giving to others that our own meager resources can be replaced with the fresh ones God wants to pour in. We are created for connection, for relationships. Relationships are maintained by a continual mutual flow of giving to one another. That interplay of love washes out the canker of selfishness and produces blessings.

This principle is illustrated by a story I heard of a woman who grew increasingly angry and embittered at her husband because of his indifference, insensitivity, and resistance to her deepest needs. She decided that divorce was the only way out and secretly consulted a lawyer.

"Not only do I want to divorce that brute," she told him, "I want it to hurt him deeply. I want to make him suffer like he's made me suffer for these past five years."

The lawyer understood and offered an ingenious plan that would hurt the man far beyond anything she had thought of. "Go back home," he said, "and don't tell your husband that you are going to divorce him. Spend the next two months treating him like a king. Do everything he loves to do. Cook his favorite meals. Cater to his every whim. Listen when he talks. Even laugh at his jokes. Go fishing and golfing with him and pretend you're having a great time. Act the part of the most loving and obedient wife on the planet. Then when he starts thinking you're the brightest jewel in the crown of ideal womanhood, I'll have all the papers ready and you can slap him in the face with the divorce. He will be devastated. Losing you will be the worst calamity that ever fell on him. He will grieve his loss for the rest of his life."

The woman was delighted with the plan. She swallowed her disgust at pretending something she didn't feel and followed the lawyer's advice in every detail. At the end of the two months, he called her and said the divorce papers were ready to serve.

"Divorce? I don't want a divorce!" she replied. "You wouldn't believe how much my husband has changed in these past two months. I don't know what came over him. He's become the most attentive, loving, and caring person I've ever known. I never in my wildest dreams thought a marriage could be this happy."

What happened here is no mystery, is it? Even though her motives were devious, for two months this woman emptied herself of self. She focused solely on the other person. The unexpected result was that her husband responded by opening himself to her. He also began to give freely. They discovered what her wise lawyer knew. (Yes, there is such a thing as a wise lawyer!) The key to real blessings and true happiness is giving first with no expectation of receiving in return. And when both partners found themselves giving freely, love and joy blossomed. Blessings flowed.

I wish I could just pray my blessing over people and *poof!*—suddenly all the hurting marriages and dysfunctional families out there would be healed. But it doesn't work that way. There's no magic in simply praying a blessing. I just hope that calling people's attention to God's desire to bless will lead them to seek his will in their lives and find the power to change in ways that will enable them to receive his blessing.

BLESSING YOUR FAMILY

As a father, there's one thing I can do to pass along the backyard blessings of marriage and family. I can put every ounce of ability and energy I have into instilling into my children these principles of happiness in relationships. With all my heart I want my own children to find the same kind of joy in family that I have found. How do I do that?

This is not easy in a world where the culture seems to be conspiring against you. Epidemic marriage failure is driving today's young people to live together instead of marrying. This, in turn, has driven the illegitimate birthrate almost to 50 percent. These children grow up without models for family happiness, often without any sort of Christlike example.

Even those raised by Christian parents and regularly taken to church are leaving the church in droves. Without principles to guide them, they are vulnerable to the pitfalls of the entertainment culture, which inevitably exposes them to sensuality and perversion. The proliferation of iPods, social websites, and smart phones often closes them off into a world of electronic communication that can effectively separate them from parental influence. Subverted by godless worldviews in public schools and unbelieving professors in college, they are easily seduced into the godless thinking of today.

To counter this formidable onslaught against the family, parents must be intentional, vigilant, and committed. It must start early. In those first years when parents have their kids' attention and respect, the groundwork must be laid for what is right and wrong, allowable and not. They must show their love by being willing to discipline. It's not always easy, but parents must stick to their guns. Deb and I have been blessed with five *great* kids. But even the most well-behaved child needs to develop a strong sense of right and wrong. This means there are certain things other kids do that your kids can't. Places other kids go that yours can't.

All this must be balanced with what they can do. Give them your time. Children spell love, T-I-M-E. This doesn't mean just "quality time." That's a myth. The *quantity* of time is really more important, even if you're not doing anything exciting or meaningful while you're together. It's not as hard as we think. Take them with you on your errands. Have fun with them while working together. Plan excursions. Movies, concerts, and plays are okay, but also expose them to the great outdoors. Go hiking. Play baseball. Take them fishing. Spread a quilt on the grass on a summer night and spend an hour or so gazing at the backyard blessing of a sky full of stars.

Early on, show them the nature of God through his creation. Teach them to love it. Lead them to understand that the best things in life are free. You can't buy more spectacular sights than great mountains, multicolored sunsets, billowing clouds, migrating bird formations, a field of flowers accented with flitting butterflies. If these things seem trite to kids today (and to adults as well), it's because we've allowed the overstimulation of popular culture to dull our sensitivity to natural, everyday wonders that are truly spectacular.

In our culture of inverted values, God's creation is to most people a place to escape to for a few days before coming back to the *real* world where the true action is. That outlook brings our task with our families into focus. We must make God's world real to them. We must show them that what comes from him is the true reality. I'm not talking just about nature; I'm speaking of moral values, integrity, selfless love, respect for others, sacrificial living, and commitment to God and his truth. That's the family blessing you want to pass on to your children.

The bottom line is this: we must educate our kids in addition to what the schools and churches do. Make your love for them and for God visible and real. Don't just teach it; live it before them in a way that they absorb it. Don't just tell your children; *show* them what living holy is like.

Families that learn to do this successfully will find the blessing of God's grace upon their home. It will be a sanctuary of rest and renewal, a haven of peace where sounds of joy and laughter grace its walls, where love and unconditional acceptance of one another is the rule.

That is the blessing I pray for you and your family.

CHAPTER 6

The Prayer for
Spiritual Victory

MAY GOD GIVE YOU THE SPIRITUAL STRENGTH TO
OVERCOME THE EVIL ONE AND AVOID TEMPTATION.
MAY GOD'S GRACE BE UPON YOU TO FULFILL YOUR
DREAMS AND VISIONS. MAY GOODNESS AND
MERCY FOLLOW YOU
ALL THE DAYS OF YOUR LONG LIFE.

WHEN I FIRST WALKED INTO the earthquake-stricken city of Port Au Prince in Haiti, I was overwhelmed by the enormity of the disaster. Most of the buildings were reduced to rubble, spilling tons of stone and concrete into the streets and blocking thoroughfares. The few structures left standing had crumbling walls and collapsed roofs, many listing sideways like sinking ships.

My heart was wrenched by the agonized cries of those still trapped in the rubble, ringing above the grinding and scraping of bulldozers and cranes moving away slabs of concrete to uncover more victims. I saw masses of bodies laid in the streets and watched as anguished people wandered among them, looking for missing loved ones. And I could not help but tear up at the wails of grief I heard when they found what they feared they would find. The smell of death filled the air everywhere I went.

In the face of such enormous, overwhelming need, a wave of hopelessness washed over me. The problems were too many, too great to handle. How could anyone even make a dent in the enormity of the task?

That sense of futility is what many people feel in the face of their own problems. I hear stories of hopelessly tangled and ruptured family relationships, of crushing debts that stretch far beyond all possibility of repayment, and of addictions that snare people early and slowly tighten the noose, strangling their will to resist. Many tell me they have tried everything, and they see no way out. They are spiritually defeated.

Those were the kinds of thoughts that ran through my head when I landed in Haiti. Yet in spite of my misgivings about meeting the enormity of that stricken country's needs, I saw evidence of the possibility that they could be met.

It came in the form of the men and women of the U.S. military, who were not only there to keep the peace at large but also to care for individuals. Their compassion struck me as they dealt with the hurting people around them, giving each one their full attention. They knew their mission, and they were focused on how to accomplish it. It also came in the form of the volunteers of

Samaritan's Purse. I remember walking into one of their medical clinics and watching them use their skills and tools to meet the many needs that came their way one at a time. The people of that broken city came into the clinic battered and bruised, but they left with a renewed sense of hope because of the attention they had received from someone who cared.

Soon the impossibility of the overall task faded as I observed these servants focus on addressing the single need that presented itself to them at the moment. As they moved from one need to another, I realized that the magnitude of the disaster was not their concern. When enough people met enough of those individual needs, the entire scope of the disaster would, in time, be dealt with.

Overwhelming us with the enormity of our problems is one of Satan's most effective strategies for spiritual defeat. "This mountain is too high for you," he says. "And look at how steep and rugged it is. Surely you can't climb that! What's the point in even trying?" So we allow the enemy's discouraging voice to discount the power of the Holy Spirit in our lives, and we give up at the outset, defeated before we even begin.

The problem you face may be an addiction, such as to alcohol, drugs, porn, or gambling. Or it may be an ingrained habit such as anger, negativity, criticism, or gossip. It may be a strong temptation to buy things you don't need and can't afford, or to cheat on your spouse. It may be a person who is a continual thorn in your side. Or your need may be something missing in your life that you want to add—a mate, an education, children, a job. Maybe your need is self-discipline to set aside time for regular prayer and Bible study, or serving your church or community in some way.

Any of these needs can loom high and steep as an alpine peak. The way to spiritual victory is not to take on the whole mountain at once but to take it on in smaller, doable chunks. Set your sights first on the lowest ridge. Climb to that level, then work your way up to the second ridge. The process may be slow, but by taking one ridge at a time, you'll find yourself at the top sooner than you might think.

THE POWER OF WORDS

A few people who could not go to Haiti told me they desperately wanted to help in some way, and they asked what they could do. I suggested that they send a check to the relief effort. I also asked them to pray, diligently and often. Pray that trapped people would be rescued quickly; that people would find their loved ones alive; that relief would come in time to save those who were without food, water, and shelter; that the city would soon be restored to order.

I am continually amazed at the enormous compliment God gives us in hearing our prayers. It simply astounds me that the greatest being in the universe wants us involved in placing his power where it's most needed. We have a solemn duty to apply that power in blessing others by offering heartfelt words to God in prayer on behalf of those who have needs.

There is another way your words can have an extremely positive effect. When the apostle Paul told believers to "encourage one another and build each other up," he was urging the church to take advantage of the power of words as a way of blessing others not only through prayer, but directly, face-to-face (1 Thess. 5:11). You *can* affect people positively with your words—not only your family, friends, and coworkers, but even people you don't know. You do it all the time. And so do I.

Sometimes I'm tempted to think a few words of encouragement are such a small drop in the full bucket of some people's problems as to be almost meaningless. But that is definitely not the case.

Make no mistake about it; you and I have far more power to bless and influence than we can ever imagine, even with what appear to be the most insignificant acts. Many of the people we live and work around are bogged down in a world of negativity in which almost all the words they hear are demeaning and belittling, barbed with criticism, put-downs, and cursing. They hear little or no encouragement, and their outlook on life is affected. For many of these people, this negativity seeps in and becomes their outlook. And they can hardly help passing it on to others.

You may not know who these people are, but you encounter them everywhere you go. You carry within you an enormous power to bless these people in small ways that could become a factor in turning their lives around. And you can do much of it just by your words.

You can bless in the way you treat the store clerk who offers you help, the mechanic who repairs your car, the waitress who takes your order, or the checker at the grocery store. Simple words of kindness and cheer that may seem such little things to you can break through the grayness of their lives like beams of sunlight, showing them that life can be brighter than what they've known.

A high school freshman—we'll call him Justin—was known to be a party animal. One day he saw a nerdy-looking boy walking home from school. He passed the boy by, wondering why he was carrying home so many of his schoolbooks on a Friday. Suddenly a bunch of boys ran toward the nerd, taunting him, tearing the books from his arms, knocking him into the dirt, and sending his glasses flying.

Justin started to walk on, but when he saw the sadness and hurt in the boy's eyes, he turned, lifted him up, found his glasses, and helped him carry his books home. On the way he learned that the boy, whom we'll call Kyle, was a new transfer from a private school and had no friends. Feeling sorry for the kid, Justin invited him to come over and play football.

Over the next four years the two boys became fast friends. On graduation, Kyle was valedictorian of the class. Justin was a little jealous, but he hid it.

As Kyle began his valedictory address, Justin was stunned by his opening remarks. In thanking the people who had helped him through school, he told of the incident in which he had first met Justin. Overcome by loneliness and being the constant victim of bullies, he had decided to end his life that weekend. But not wanting his mother to have to clean out his locker, he was carrying all his books home when Justin's kind words turned him away from doing the unspeakable.

Kyle went on to become a medical doctor. Healed by the power of kind words and friendship, he became a healer to others.[1]

THE BUTTERFLY EFFECT

As the story of Justin and Kyle shows, the small flashes of light we beam into the lives of others can have more meaning than we think. It's an example of what some physicists call the "butterfly effect." In short, the butterfly effect says that the amount of air displaced by a butterfly's wings can eventually generate a hurricane. No, they're not talking about some monstrous mutant butterfly. They mean that small movements of air cause other small movements, and those movements combine to build momentum and create larger movements until finally enough of these movements accumulate to generate winds of hurricane force.

You may bless someone in a small way that you think nothing about. Your blessing causes that person to take a given action, which in turn affects two or three others. Those three go on to affect six more, who in turn affect twelve others, until a family, a community, a city, a state, or a nation is turned around.

The way that a single blessing can grow to affect thousands is illustrated in the story of Hilde Back, a Holocaust survivor who sent fifteen dollars per month to Kenya to fund a child's education. It was a small gesture for Hilde, but it had a big impact on the life of Chris Mburu, the Kenyan boy who received her help. Because of her consistent monthly funding, Chris was able to get through high school and earn a scholarship to Harvard. On graduation from Harvard, he became a successful attorney for the U.N.

Mr. Mburu never forgot the gift that made his success possible, and in his gratitude he founded a scholarship fund for deprived children who would otherwise never receive the education that so blessed him. And he named the fund for his benefactor, Hilde Back.[2]

We never know the long-range impact of our deeds, words, or examples. We have the ability to affect people daily, not only through small acts of kindness but simply through the way we live. That is why it is critical that you and I strive to live in holiness every moment. Who we are and what we do impacts our family, coworkers, friends, store clerks, waitresses, even people passing you in the mall or dining at the table next to yours.

You even have the power to bless in the way you drive on the freeway. Either you show an example of courtesy to others and respect for the law, or you don't. You set a positive example or you set off anger, either of which may be passed on to others with effects far beyond what you might imagine. You can't escape your potential for blessing.

For people who are in the public eye, this responsibility is inescapable. I am not only onstage in my concerts, where it's obvious I must take care to reflect God's Spirit, but people are watching me everywhere I go. They say, "Michael W. Smith claims to be a God follower. Let's see if he really walks the walk."

Fair or not, people in the public eye tend to become role models for others, and they cannot just wear one face onstage and then drop it when the curtain falls. This can be a real problem, because their temptations can be so much greater. If their public visibility has gone to their heads and swollen their egos, they are highly vulnerable to yielding to those temptations and ruining their influence and potential to bless.

We're all aware of influential people, both inside and outside the church, who projected a moral, wholesome image but found themselves trapped in a sinful lifestyle. When we hear of these behaviors, we mourn the loss of their positive influence. Their capacity to use their social position for blessing is diminished, and we hurt for them.

Celebrities and people of spiritual influence may have the greater responsibility, and they may be more vulnerable to temptation. But the truth is, we all share this responsibility and this vulnerability. If you are a Christ follower, the evil one is after you. When you signed on for Christ, you enlisted in a great war. You became a combatant in a titanic battle for spiritual dominion that has been going on since before Adam and Eve. The enemy has marked you for annihilation, and his demonic armies are aiming their big guns right at your heart.

Satan wants you to stumble and fall. He wants your failure to cause others to think that Christianity is empty of meaning and powerless to change lives. If he can tempt you to forget whose side you're on just for a moment—that moment when the waitress gets your order wrong, or when your child is bugging you with a homework question while you're glued to the TV with your team three points behind and on the opponent's two-yard line with eighteen seconds to play, or when your wife is out of town and that curvy sales assistant with the low-cut dress is flirting with you—if Satan can get you to forget your commitment to holiness for just that moment, he may bring down not only you, but others who are watching you. It's a serious thing to be a follower of Jesus. We must find ourselves in a state of constant dependency on him. We must ask God for his strength to overcome the evil one and resist such temptations.

BLESSING YOUR NEIGHBOR

As you can see, I firmly believe in the power of words to bless people. As I've said, it's not because of any magic in the words themselves. It's because of their power in conveying your care and love.

But I wouldn't be telling you the whole truth if I left you with the impression that words alone are always adequate. There is a time for words, and there is a time for action. As James tells us:

> Suppose you see a brother or sister who has no food or clothing, and you say, "Good-bye and have a good day; stay warm and eat well"—but then you don't give that person any food or clothing. What good does that do? (James 2:15–16 NLT)

The apostle Paul told us to make it a habit to be encouragers (1 Thess. 5:11). This is a way of blessing people we encounter, even when we know nothing about them or their needs. James, on the other hand, is saying, "Don't resort to mere words of encouragement when you encounter people facing a visible need for hands-on help." He's warning us against being all talk when it's obvious that action is needed.

Blessing with words should be a policy that we follow in all our dealings with people in general. Blessing with actions applies specifically to those tangible needs that God places in front of us.

We've all had experiences when we've seen a need and felt our hearts leap out of our chests—as if God himself were in us saying, "Do it for my sake." It could be an elderly neighbor across the street in need of help with the lawn, or a child on the other side of the globe who needs sponsorship through an organization like Compassion International. When we encounter a real need that we can meet personally, that's when, as James points out, words alone are not enough.

Jesus taught that the needs of our neighbor are always

our responsibility. "And who is my neighbor?" the Pharisees asked him. Jesus answered with the parable of the Good Samaritan, which shows that our neighbor is any person we come across who has a need that we have the power to meet (Luke 10:27–37). That means your family all the time. It means your friends, coworkers, and fellow believers as you see needs arise in their lives. More than that, as Jesus' parable shows, your neighbor can be anyone you encounter who has a need that you can meet. You have the power to bless these people both in word and in deed by loaning God your hands to meet their need.

About a year ago, I was running an errand on a Sunday afternoon. Along the way I saw a middle-aged man sitting at the side of the road. His clothes were dirty, and the expression on his face gave away the heaviness that he carried in his heart. He was holding a sign asking for food. I was compelled to help, so I pulled into the nearest fast-food place and ordered something. His eyes lifted as I pulled up and got out of the car, as if he was surprised that I was there. I gave him the food that I had ordered and sat down to talk with him for a while. He shared that he had spent the morning sitting near the entrance to a church nearby. His words were saturated with bitterness as he explained that none of the people who left the entrance of the church that morning had given him a second glance. My heart ached, and I offered an apology.

This man didn't know who I was, nor did I know who he was. And I'm quite sure that the fast food that I offered him wasn't going to solve all of his problems. But the simple fact that someone showed him compassion in the form of food and a kind word moved him. He hadn't experienced kindness from anyone for quite a while. He ate his food and expressed his thanks as I went on my way.

DESIRING A BLESSING

We've spent most of this book talking about how Christ followers should focus not on themselves but on blessing others. And we've shown how blessing others inevitably results in blessings for ourselves. God blesses us in proportion to how we open our hands to receive his blessing, and how open our hands remain in passing on his blessings to those who need them.

In these final pages I want to assure you that it's not wrong for you to desire a blessing for yourself. Remember Jacob? He went so far as to wrestle with God for a personal blessing. And he got it (Gen. 32:24–30).

God wants to bless you as much as you want to be blessed. Let's face it: we all need blessing. It's part of our lot in this fallen world to have hurts and needs. And it's part of God's intention for us to have dreams and aspirations that we desire to have fulfilled. We naturally want God's blessings to see us through our hurts and to fulfill those dreams.

I pray that God will bless you by fulfilling your dreams. At the same time, I pray that your dreams will rise higher than career success or wealth or pleasure. I hope you will open yourself to God's blessing by dreaming the dream God has for you. He is your Maker, and he made you as a unique being with attributes and abilities that make you different from any other person ever created. He made you this way because he has a function for you to fulfill that you can do better than any other person on earth. He wants to bless you by putting you in a place where you can fulfill it.

This means that when we pray for God's blessing, we are praying for God to put us where he intended for us to be, doing what he intended for us to do. If we work against God's intention, we will be working against the blessing he wants to give. If a fish were to dream of soaring among the clouds like an eagle, I'm pretty sure God would not bless that dream. God didn't equip a fish to fly. Our dreams must match God's purpose for our lives.

Sometimes God's purpose is not immediately clear to us. Many people live in frustration because they cannot find the place where they seem to fit. How do we find that place? Sometimes it shows up clearly in our talents and our desires. The first time I sat at a piano, something clicked in my soul, and I knew what I was meant to do. But for many others, the path is foggy and obscure. And the reasons can vary. I believe that many unintentionally bury God's intent for them under ambitions they pick up from the surrounding culture. In a wealth-and-success-oriented society, it's easy for one's ambitions to follow the popular concept of success and miss out on the higher and happier life God wants to give you.

If the path to that higher and happier life is not clear,

you can take positive steps toward finding it. You can pray for guidance and then tune your spirit to hear the answer by spending time in God's Word and quiet meditation. You can seek the counsel of trusted Christian mentors. Committed friends who know you and have your well-being at heart can often see things about you that are not clear to yourself.

When you ask for the blessing of having your dreams fulfilled, it's important that you get on the same page with God. If he gave you fins, you face only frustration if you pursue a dream that requires wings. A person who stands four foot eleven should not dream of playing in the NBA. Nor should a person who stands six foot six dream of being a racehorse jockey. To be truly blessed, you must set your sights on what God has equipped you to be.

"But," you may say, "I've always wanted to be a doctor. What if God wants me to be an accountant? I hate working with figures. Doesn't God want me to be joyful in my Christian life? How can I be joyful doing something I hate?"

Well, I don't think God will ask you to do something

you truly hate. It's likely he will put into your heart a desire to do what he intends for you. Sometimes that desire may be buried, and you may need to dig it out from under all the other desires you've heaped on top of it. That's where prayer and counsel come into play.

I think we can safely say that you'll never find joy in making yourself into something God didn't intend. You will find joy only in being all he wants you to be. The apostle Paul gives us the key in Romans 8:28: "And we know that God causes everything to work together for the good of those who love God *and are called according to his purpose for them*" (NLT; emphasis added). God has a purpose for you, and he calls you to it. If you don't hear that call, the way to receive the blessing it promises is to clear from your mind the clutter of your own desires. Then pray, counsel, and listen until God's will becomes clear.

I do not presume to know God's purpose for your life. You may be given talents that call you to the ministry or to some profession or trade. But wherever God puts you, I am sure of this: he wants to bless you. And he wants you to bless others through his gifts to you. That is the only way your dreams and visions can be fulfilled.

Submit to God's will for you, and you can be sure that goodness and mercy will follow you all the days of your life, and you will dwell in the house of the Lord forever.

THE LORD BLESS YOU, AND KEEP YOU;
THE LORD MAKE HIS FACE SHINE
   ON YOU, AND BE GRACIOUS TO YOU;
THE LORD LIFT UP HIS COUNTENANCE
   ON YOU, AND GIVE YOU PEACE.
      —NUMBERS 6:24–26 NASB

Notes

Chapter 5: The Prayer for Backyard Blessings

1. Michael W. Smith, "Agnus Dei" (New York: Sony/ATV Milene Music), 1990.

Chapter 6: The Prayer for Spiritual Victory

1. Adapted from "Inspirational Short Story: The Power of Words," by an anonymous author on the Circles of Light website: http://www.circlesoflight.com/articles/word-power.shtml.

2. Adapted from "'A Small Act,' Director Jennifer Arnold, 'Be Prepared for Anything'" on the website of IndieWire: http://www.indiewire.com/article/laff_10_a_small_act_director_jennifer_arnold_be_prepared_for_anything/.

In addition to winning several Grammy and Dove awards, **Michael W. Smith** has recorded more than 25 albums and had numerous hit radio songs in the Christian and general markets. He is also involved in mission work at home and around the world, and is the founder of Rocketown, an outreach to teenagers in a 38,000 square-foot facility in downtown Nashville, Tennessee. He has written several bestselling books, including *Old Enough to Know* and *Friends Are Friends Forever*. He and his wife, Debbie, have five children and live in Nashville.

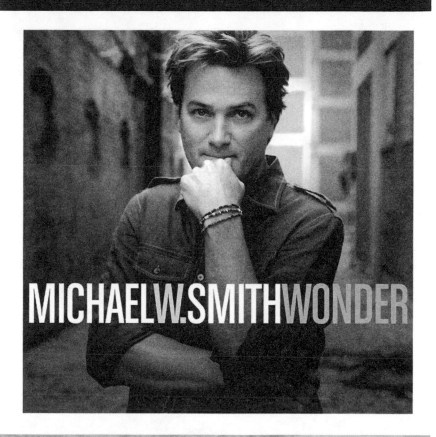

www.MICHAELWSMITH.com

:: MUSIC :: TOUR INFO :: NEWS :: COMMUNITY ::

www.FACEBOOK.com/MICHAELWSMITHOFFICIAL

www.TWITTER.com/MICHAELWSMITH

Share Your Thoughts

With the Author: Your comments will be forwarded to the author when you send them to *zauthor@zondervan.com*.

With Zondervan: Submit your review of this book by writing to *zreview@zondervan.com*.

Free Online Resources at
www.zondervan.com

Zondervan AuthorTracker: Be notified whenever your favorite authors publish new books, go on tour, or post an update about what's happening in their lives at www.zondervan.com/authortracker.

Daily Bible Verses and Devotions: Enrich your life with daily Bible verses or devotions that help you start every morning focused on God. Visit www.zondervan.com/newsletters.

Free Email Publications: Sign up for newsletters on Christian living, academic resources, church ministry, fiction, children's resources, and more. Visit www.zondervan.com/newsletters.

Zondervan Bible Search: Find and compare Bible passages in a variety of translations at www.zondervanbiblesearch.com.

Other Benefits: Register yourself to receive online benefits like coupons and special offers, or to participate in research.

ZONDERVAN®

ZONDERVAN.com/
AUTHORTRACKER
follow your favorite authors